BOEING
THE WORLD'S GREATEST PLANEMAKERS

CHARTWELL
BOOKS, INC.

Published by Chartwell Books Inc.
A division of Book Sales Inc.
110 Enterprise Avenue,
Secaucus, New Jersey 07094.

ISBN 0 89009 532 9

Printed in Hong Kong

Produced by Winchmore Publishing Services Limited.
48 Lancaster Avenue,
Hadley Wood, Herts.

Edited by Sue Butterworth
Designed by Pierre Tilley and Andrzej Bielecki
Picture Research by Jonathan and Diane Moore

CONTENTS

THE INFANT GIANT

IT WAS TWO AMERICANS, Orville and Wilbur Wright, who made the world's first successful flight in a heavier-than-air craft on 17 December 1903. But the enormous lead that this should have given the USA and its many aviation enthusiasts was wasted for a variety of reasons, and the Europeans rapidly became the world leaders in powered flight. But aviation did flourish in the USA, largely through exhibition flights and race meetings, though it was soon clear to all that American aircraft were technically worse then the European machines, even if flown with skill. It was also notable that American pilots were often very reckless, a style of flying that became even more common in the barnstorming days after the First World War.

It was into this gap between the enthusiasm of pilot and the backward aircraft coming from US manufacturers that William E. Boeing stepped in 1915. Based at Seattle in the state of Washington, Boeing was a prominent local man with interests in land and timber. During 1915, in the course of conversations with his friend Commander Conrad Westervelt, an officer of the US Navy attached to a shipbuilding yard in Seattle, Boeing decided that the two men could design and build an aircraft with sturdier construction and better performance than the primitive machines they had seen at air exhibitions in the north-western states of the USA in recent years. Having decided to design such an aircraft in partnership with Westervelt, Boeing bought one of the latest designs available, a Martin Model T, to find out about the latest American aerodynamic and structural thinking. To house his purchase, and to provide space for the design and building of the collaborative aircraft, Boeing had built on pilings on the edge of Lake Union, in the middle of Seattle, a large hangar/factory with a slipway into the water.

Flying the Model T, and just as frequently repairing it, soon brought home to Boeing and Westervelt the problems involved in the design of a successful aircraft. However, by late 1915 the two friends felt themselves ready to start work on their first design which, not surprisingly, was desig-

nated B&W and bore more than a passing resemblance to the Model T floatplane on which the partners had gained their close acquaintance with matters aeronautical. Two examples of the B&W were built, but before the first flew in June 1916, Westervelt had been transferred to the east coast. However, the B&W floatplanes proved very successful, and Boeing was nearly able to persuade the US Navy to adopt the type as a trainer. Indeed, so enthusiastic was Boeing about the future of this new interest that on 15 July 1916 he incorporated the Pacific Aero Products Company for the manufacture of aircraft.

The new company's first venture was unsuccessful, the US Navy refusing to order a production version of the B&W. But the service was sufficiently impressed with the new company's work to urge the development of a more advanced type to meet the navy's detailed requirement for a trainer. Characteristically 'thinking big' Boeing immediately increased his company's engineering and construction facilities while pressing ahead with the design of two new types: a seaplane capable of meeting the US Navy's needs and also usable for sport or commercial operations; and a landplane suitable for US Army purchase. The seaplane was built to the total of four examples in two variants, and the landplane was built to the extent of two aircraft. Two of the Model 3 seaplanes were tested by the US Navy and then ordered into what was by the standards of the day widespread production: 50 examples of the marginally improved Model 5. Pacific Aero Products' capabilities were unequal to so large an order, and Boeing accordingly expanded his aircraft activities by turning over another of his interests, the Heath Shipyard on the Duwanish river south of Seattle (builder of the floats for the two B&Ws), to the manufacture of aircraft. Many of the shipyard's facilities proved well suited to the conversion, and further expansion was possible on

William Boeing (with mailbag) and Eddie Hubbard pose in front of the Boeing CL-4S used for the world's first international air-mail service.

the same site when the US Navy sub-contracted the manufacture of 50 Curtiss HS-2L flying-boats to the Boeing Airplane Company, as Pacific Aero Products had become on 26 April 1917. This was a mere 20 days after the USA had entered the First World War on the side of the Allies, an event which resulted in a rapidly growing series of orders for US aircraft manufacturers, though the types were usually of British, French and even Italian design.

With the establishment of the Heath Shipyard facility as the Boeing Airplane Company's main manufacturing centre, the company had become established in the form it was to retain until the period immediately before the Second World War. The Lake Union facility was retained as a flight base until after the First World War, when it was sold; no flying facilities were established at the shipyard, however, for a small local airstrip was made by filling in an area some few hundred yards to the north-west of the factory, and most official testing was done at the forces' local bases: Sand

Point Naval Air Station some 10 miles to the north, and Camp Lewis some 50 miles to the south. With the growth of civil aviation in the USA after 1926, civil aircraft were tested from King County Airport on Boeing Field, only 2 miles from the shipyard. In 1936 the need for larger production facilities resulted in the building of a new factory at Boeing Field, and the original factory was then designated Plant No. 1.

One of the reasons for Boeing's receipt of an order for 50 Curtiss HS-2L flying-boats was the company's experience with waterplanes, and also its familiarity with the constructional method used by Curtiss for the hulls of these classic flying-boats (a built-up surface of criss-crossed wood veneer strips laid over wooden formers). The end of the First World War in November 1918 resulted in enormous contract cancellations throughout the expanding US aircraft industry, but Boeing escaped somewhat lightly, for 25 of the HS-2Ls were so far advanced in construction that the US Navy allowed the aircraft to be finished.

It was clear that the end of the war

Boeing's first aircraft, the B & W, was eventually sold with its sister-ship to the New Zealand government.

would also leave the armed forces with large quantities of aircraft for service in the immediate future, so Boeing wisely decided to examine the possibilities of the civil aircraft market. The result was the Boeing Model 6, a compact biplane flying-boat that made extensive use of the company's recently acquired experience with Curtiss methods of design and construction. To promote civil interest in the type, Boeing allocated the flying-boat the alternative designation B-1. Performance was excellent when flight trials were conducted in December 1919 and the beginning of 1920, but such was the impact of war-surplus military aircraft flooding the civil market that only the sole example was built at that time. The B-1 proved a sturdy machine, and was sold to Edward Hubbard for use on his air-mail route between Seattle and Victoria, British Columbia. This classic service, the world's first international air-mail route, had been inaugurated on 3 March 1919 by Hubbard and William Boeing, using the Boeing CL-4S, as the sole civil Model 5 (built for Boeing under the designation C-700) was retitled when adapted for its new role. At a time when the operational life span of a new aircraft was often measured in months, the B-1 was amazing for its longevity: Hubbard kept it in constant service until 1928.

Other civil aircraft followed: the Model 7 (BB-1) was essentially a scaled-down B-1, with seating for two passengers in addition to the pilot, but with considerably less power than the B-1; and the Model 8 (BB-L6) was in many respects a landplane version of the BB-1, with a triangular-section, mahogany plywood-covered fuselage inspired by the Ansaldo A-1 Balilla that was visiting Seattle at the time. Despite all Boeing's efforts to sell such designs in the growing civil market, no orders were forthcoming, and the company was forced to reconsider its position: the military had many thousands of aircraft, mostly of the trainer and artillery observation/reconnais-

sance types and generally still in mint condition in their delivery crates, which they were only too willing to dump on the civil market, as private-owner and joy-riding aircraft, at prices only 10 per cent (or lower) of that the manufacturers of newly-designed civil aircraft would have to charge to make a profit. It made little difference, given the difference in prices, that the purpose-designed civil aircraft were far better. So the aircraft manufacturers would not be able to enjoy the boom they had so confidently anticipated in 1919 until all the stocks of war-surplus aircraft had been used up.

What had at first seemed a rosy picture for aircraft builders was now made even blacker by the realization that production for the armed forces would also be limited in the immediate future: even allowing for the wholesale disposal of war-surplus types, the US Army and US Navy still had considerable stocks of new aircraft, which would prevent any large-scale production orders for some time. Indeed, despite the somewhat glaring gaps in the front-line aircraft inventories of

both services, the generally held belief that the First World War marked the end of major wars for some time indicated that there would be only the most limited opportunity even for prototype design.

It was a dismal period for the American aircraft manufacturers: most tried to diversify, turning their attentions to the civil market, and others simply disappeared. Boeing was relatively well placed at this time – it had won a good reputation for its skill in the making of wooden aircraft, and was located in the centre of one of the country's main wood-producing areas. The company was thus able to get by with the manufacture of non-aviation products: furniture of various kinds, canoes, and a number of Hickman Sea Sleds (powerful catamaran boats capable of many tasks).

The company's prospects began to look up again in 1920, when the US Army had been able to assess the les-

The BB-1 was a commercial and sport flying-boat, and was sold to the Aircraft Manufacturing Co. of Vancouver.

sons of the recent war in Europe and so come to the conclusion that it needed to update its forces regularly but in small numbers, to keep abreast of the latest technical developments. A feature unique to the US forces here played into Boeing's hands: when the US Army Air Service bought a prototype, it also acquired production rights to the type, and if the type seemed suitable the service called for tenders to build production batches. In this way Boeing secured an order for 200 Thomas-Morse MB-3A biplane fighters, while the original designers were galled to receive orders only for the initial 50 aircraft of the desired total of 250.

Another feature of US military aviation of this period was that both the US Army and the US Navy maintained their own design and limited construction facilities: prototypes of new types could thus be produced swiftly by the user service. If production was then required, it was allocated by the normal process of industry tender. Boeing profited from both aspects of the US Army's system: it was contracted to build 20 examples of the US Army Air Service Engineering Division's GA-1 ground-attack triplane (an ugly armoured machine, of historical interest as the last production triplane in the world), and two prototypes of the slightly more practical GA-2 ground-attack biplane. Both types were produced under the company designation Model 10, but only 10 GA-1s were built as the order was cut by half after it had been placed.

A third factor that allowed Boeing to abandon non-aeronautical work was an attractive contract to rebuild many of the DH-4/O2M series built in the First World War. These were the US Army and US Navy designations for the classic de Havilland D.H.4 which had been produced in large numbers during and immediately after the war for many roles after the type had been redesigned to acept the Liberty engine. Several manufacturers were involved in the original building and later rebuilding programmes. Boeing contributed to the latter: 111 DH-4s converted into DH-4Bs with the pilot and observer/gunner moved together by reversing the position of the pilot's

cockpit and the main fuel tank (all returned to the US Army between March and July 1920); three DH-4s converted into XDH-4M-1s with steel-tube fuselages built with the aid of a Boeing-developed arc-welding process; 147 DH-4s updated to DH-4M-1 standard and delivered between January and September 1924, mainly for photographic reconnaissance purposes; 30 DH-4s brought up to DH-4M-1 standard but delivered to the US Marine Corps as 26 O2B-1s (standard observation configuration) and four O2B-2s (airways configuration) in March 1925; and three DH-4M-1s reworked as Boeing Model 42 aircraft with revised tailplanes, tapered wings and tripod main landing gear units, and delivered to the US Army as XCO-7s in early 1925 to assess the possibility of further extension of the DH-4's service use.

While it was undertaking this work for the US Army (the 30 O2Bs for the US Marine Corps had been diverted from this source), the company had also

Left: **The GA-2 was an armoured monster, with an armament of four downward-firing machine-guns, one 37-mm cannon and two rear-defence machine-guns.**
Below left: **The GA-1 was a hopeless anachronism, with outdated layout and dismal performance allied to heavy firepower.**

variants that kept the Boeing work force well employed for some years to come, while providing the US Army and US Navy with some of its classic fighter biplanes of the late 1920s and early 1930s.

In a fashion that was to become almost standard, Boeing decided that the only way to secure orders for its new fighter aircraft was to use its own money to build a prototype with performance so superior to that of the US armed forces' current fighters that the services would order the new type in quantity. So costly a move risked all that the company had so far achieved, and much thought went into the new fighter, not only in terms of flight performance, but also in terms of potential growth (assuming the continued increase in power output from suitable engines) and serviceability. At the time of the new type's initial design, Boeing's main strength still lay with the 'traditional' wood structure, but considerable advances were being made with metal and even light alloy structures. Boeing engineers were sent to Europe to gather as much information as possible about the latest constructional thinking and methods, and the company was able to finalize its basic thinking in January 1922: the Model 15 stuck to the current aerodynamic concepts and the same 300-hp Wright-Hispano Model H inline piston engine as used in the MB-3A, but adopted the type of structure pioneered by the talented German designer, Reinhold Platz, in a number of Fokker designs (most notably the D VII fighter that had so impressed the American air forces in 1918 and during post-war evaluation in the USA): semi-cantilever wood wings based on a deep aerofoil section that permitted strong box spars, and a welded steel-tube fuselage. The Model 15 was modelled closely on the D VII, but introduced a number of features desirable on a fighter intended for the US Army Air Service. Significant alterations after the initial design had been planned were the substitution of semi-cantilever spars for fully cantilever units (and the introduction of wire bracing as a result), alteration from untapered to tapered wing panels, replacement of the Wright-Hispano Model H with the new

built three TB-1 torpedo-bombers for the US Navy. These were to an improved design that the Naval Aircraft Factory had evolved from the Martin T3M, itself a company-inspired development of the NAF's SC series, which had been built by both Curtiss and Martin: such were the design and production swings of the period. The three TB-1s were produced under the Boeing designation Model 63, and when delivered in 1927 these were the last aircraft not designed by Boeing to

be delivered from Seattle until the Second World War.

These tasks had seen the company through the difficult period of the early 1920s, and had also allowed the development of new constructional techniques as well as providing useful insights into the thinking and methods of other manufacturers and of the armed forces. But Boeing was now ready once more to step forward with a design of its own; and from this one basic design concept flowed a host of

435-hp Curtiss D-12 inline, and relocation of the coolant radiator from a frontal position to a tunnel position under the engine in a format that became a hallmark of American fighters in the late 1920s.

During 1922 Boeing began construction of the prototype Model 15, and so attractive was the design that the US Army offered to supply the engine, armament and other items of purely military equipment in return for the right to evaluate the aircraft. Under the new military designation system the Model 15 was designated XPW-9, and made its first flight on 2 June 1923 in the hands of Captain Frank Tyndall, the USAAC pilot attached to the company. Following initial flight trials at Seattle, the XPW-9 was moved by rail to McCook Field for USAAC evaluation against contemporary types. Service tests confirmed the superiority of the Boeing fighter's tunnel radiator and tapered wings: by another turn of the wheel such a radiator was retrospectively applied with beneficial results on the competing Curtiss XPW-8A, which was redesignated XPW-8B when it was also fitted with tapered wings. In this way the XPW-8B benefitted from Boeing's design thinking to become the true precursor of the amazingly successful and prolific Curtiss Hawk series of fighters, which first appeared in 1925 as the US Army's P-1.

The US Army was impressed by the XPW-9 as a complete aircraft as well as for its individual new features, and so ordered two XPW-9s of its own. These aircraft were very similar to the original Model 15, but the second introduced a new type of landing gear arrangement, with divided main units replacing the earlier through-axle type, and this became standard on production examples of Boeing's Model 15. The qualities of the new type were clear to the US Navy as well as the US Army, and production for both services was ordered: of a total of 77 Model 15 main-run aircraft, 61 went to the US Army as PW-9s (one being diverted to the National Advisory

The TB-1 torpedo-bomber was built by Boeing but designed by the Naval Aircraft Factory, and was later developed into the Douglas T2D-1.

Committee for Aeronautics, and another becoming the prototype XP-4) and 16 to the US Navy as FB-1s, intended for land- rather than ship-based operations. But this was only the beginning of the story, even for the basic Model 15. In 1925 the US Army ordered 25 of the improved Model 15A under the designation PW-9A, the last of the batch being completed as the sole PW-9B (Model 15B) with the more powerful D-12D engine; there followed 40 production examples of the PW-9C with the uprated power-plant, stronger fuselage and other detail improvements, built under the company designation Model 15C; and 16 of the final US Army variant, the PW-9D (Model 15D) with many modifications to improve safety, as well as a rudder of increased area. The last PW-9D was converted into the proto-type XP-7 (Boeing Model 93). The US Navy had also pressed ahead with limited purchases of improved variants of the basic FB: two FB-2s (Model 53s) intended for carrier operations, and so fitted with arrester hooks, through-axle landing gears with guide

hooks for the longitudinal deck wires; two FB-3s (Model 55s), plus one conversion from FB-1 standard, intended for floatplane operation, and so fitted with hoisting gear and twin-float landing gears; one FB-4 (Model 54) based on the FB-1 but with the floats of the FB-3, and powered by the new 450-hp Wright P-1 radial engine, whose poor performance resulted in the substitution of the 400-hp Pratt & Whitney Wasp radial, under the revised designation FB-6; and the major production variant of the FB series, the FB-5 (Model 67), of which 27 were built for delivery in January 1927. This last variant had a number of improvements over its predecessors, and was powered by the 520-hp Packard 2A-1500 inline engine, an updated version of the engine which had powered the FB-3s. Despite the excellent performance of the FB-5s, the type served with the US Navy as a first-line fighter for only two years, the service deciding in 1929 to standardize on radial engines, which were lighter and less complex, for all its shipboard aircraft.

The basic soundness of the design

The PW-9D was a classic biplane fighter, and introduced several refinements including a balanced rudder.

that originated with the Model 15 is in no way better proved than by the number of production variants developed from it, and also in the variety of experimental models to spring from the same line: the XP-4 (Model 58) had a turbocharged Packard engine of 510 hp; the XP-8 (Model 66) was powered by the 2A-1500 inverted inline engine with its radiator set into the centre section of the lower wing; the AT-3 (Model 68) was an experimental single-seat advanced trainer converted from a PW-9A by the substitution of a 180-hp Wright-Hispano Model E engine in place of the standard Curtiss D-12; and the XP-7 (Model 93) was the final PW-9D fitted with the 600-hp Curtiss Conqueror inline engine.

Production of the MB-3A, modification of the DH-4 series, and production of the Model 15 and its derivatives had now put Boeing back into a relatively secure position as an aircraft constructor. It was now the company's problem

to keep up this momentum, and here the basic flexibility and growth potential of the Model 15 proved its value: the primary modifications that had led to the wide-ranging PW-9/FB series now gave way to secondary adaptations that resulted in yet further models, whose production examples were delivered principally to the US Navy. The starting point for this series of developments was the Boeing Model 69, which was ordered in prototype form by the US Navy as the XF2B-1 in 1926. The airframe of the XF2B-1 was modelled on that of the XP-8, while the powerplant and its installation were closely similar to those of the FB-6. Prototype evaluation of this Wasp-powered prototype was successful, and the US Navy accordingly ordered 32 of the production version, designated F2B-1 but retaining the same company designation as the prototype despite the removal of the propeller spinner and the substitution of a horn-balanced rudder in place of the prototype's plain unit. Two further examples were built for export under the company designation Model 69-B. Next to

appear, in March 1927, was the Model 74, which was tested by the US Navy as the XF3B-1: this was in fact the airframe of the F2B fitted with the landing gear of the FB-5, but it could also be fitted with a float gear (single main unit and two balancer units) for maritime operations. US Navy interest in this variant was only short-lived, and Boeing therefore remodelled the type completely as the Model 77. This retained the basic fuselage and engine of the Model 74, though the nose was lengthened; but the wings, landing gear and tail unit were entirely new. The wings were swept back slightly untapered, while the tail unit was designed round a new semi-monocoque principle in which stiffness was given to the all-metal structure by the use of corrugated metal skinning. (A semi-monocoque structure is one in which the skinning, supported by light internal formers and stringers, bears the basic structural load. In earlier structures the load was taken by an internal unit of longerons and spacers, braced inside by wire and covered by fabric to provide a 'smooth' external

finish.) The same 435-hp Pratt & Whitney Wasp engine was retained, but the new design was operationally more versatile than its predecessors, and despite having a bomb load of only five 25-lb bombs, it was described as a fighter-bomber. The Model 77 first flew in February 1928, and production of 73 F3B-1s followed soon afterwards, deliveries to the US Navy being made between August and November of the same year. In the following year 18 of the F3B-1s were converted into shipboard light bombers for the use of a squadron aboard the carrier USS *Saratoga*.

It should not be imagined that all Boeing's design efforts were centred upon the Model 15 and its immediate descendents during the mid-1920s. Indeed, the period from 1923 to 1929 was quite prolific so far as Boeing designs were concerned, with a number of types intended for the civil aviation market complementing the company's

efforts directed towards the US Army and US Navy. The trouble was that in the early 1920s airlines were not permitted by US law, so civil aircraft had to cater for the needs of private owners, with all the resulting problems of small production runs and high unit costs. At the same time the company was partially hampered by the attitudes of US buyers: they would not consider a totally new design, which usually suited Boeing but was now in part a difficulty as the company was starting to move away from its tradition of evolutionary designs and reliance on accepted constructional practice, modified only slowly to meet customer acceptance rather than designer insistence.

Two of the keys to the re-emergence of the US aircraft industry as a world force appeared in 1926: firstly, it

was announced that from 1927 the US Post Office would call for bids for the nation's air-mail sectors, as the government had decided to allow commercial operation of these routes in place of the current government-operated service; and secondly, the radial engine finally came into its own with the appearance of the Pratt & Whitney Wasp. This engine offered a power output greater than that of the First World War Liberty engine, but at a considerably reduced weight: being a radial engine it did not require all the radiator and all the plumbing of inline engines, and was (exclusive of the radiator etc) still more than 200 lb lighter than the Liberty. So the difference in weight between the two engines of comparable power gave the aircraft designer a useful advantage: with the radial engine he

A wary-looking passenger peers from the cramped two-passenger cabin that made the Model 40A such a success.

could use the weight saving to give his aircraft the ability to carry the same payload over a longer range, or to carry a larger payload over the same range. Whichever option was chosen, the radial engine offered far better operating economics.

Boeing was one of the first Americans to grasp fully what was offered by the radial engine, which had been used first in a Boeing aircraft to power the FB-6. The company immediately set about the design of a military aircraft tailored to the Wasp radial (this appearing as the XF2B-1), but also considered methods of applying the engine to civil aircraft. Early in 1925 Boeing had produced to the require-

ments of the Post Office Department a possible replacement for the mail-plane version of the Liberty-engined DH-4. The specification demanded the use of a Liberty engine, and the Boeing Model 40 was a workmanlike response that failed (as did the other contenders) because of the limitations of its engine. However, the opening up of air-mail routes to civil operators spurred Boeing to redesign the Model 40 into the Wasp-powered Model 40A: this not only possessed better performance than its competitors, but also allowed two passengers to be carried, and the fares of these two would add to the operator's income from the carriage of air-mail. The facts speak for themselves: powered by a 400-hp Liberty engine, the Model 40 could carry 1,000 lb of mail over 700 miles; powered by a 420-hp Wasp, the

Model 40A could carry 1,200 lb of mail and two passengers over 650 miles. Given the totally superior operating economics of his Model 40A aircraft, Boeing was able to tender a bid some 50 per cent lower than any other for the San Francisco – Chicago sector of the transcontinental mail route. Other bidders thought that Boeing had hopelessly underbid for the route, which is not surprising given that their own bids were based on aircraft that could not compete with the Model 40A, and the new Boeing Air Transport Corporation was awarded the contract, based on the use of 24 Model 40As, the twenty-fifth aircraft being delivered to Pratt & Whitney as a test-bed for the Wasp and future radial engines. Boeing was able to steal this march over his competitors as a result of his excellent relationship with Frederick Rent-

A Model 40A at Reno, Nevada, the second stop out from San Francisco on the air-mail route to Chicago.

schler, president of Pratt & Whitney: Wasps were in very short supply, and Boeing was able to use engines destined for F2B-1s on Rentschler's personal assurance that more Wasps would be delivered by the time the fighters were nearly ready for them.

The US government's acceptance of Boeing's air-mail bid introduced a totally new era for the company, but it must not be forgotten that during this period the development of other aircraft for strictly commercial purposes had not ceased. Next to appear after the original Model 15 was the Model 21, a primary trainer designed to meet a US Navy requirement. The structure was based on that of the Model 15, but

several relatively new features were included: the upper and lower wing panels were interchangeable, so easing stores holding problems; N-struts for interplane bracing removed the need for incidence bracing wires; and a divided-axle landing gear arrangement was used from the start. Power was provided by a 200-hp Lawrance J-1 radial, and the prototype was at first found unsuitable for the US Navy's needs as it was too good an aircraft: it was too easy to handle and could not be put into a spin. Modifications were made, and 41 production examples were ordered by the US Navy under the designation NB-1. These were fitted with Lawrance J-1, J-2 and J-4 radials, and the survivors were later re-engined with 220-hp Wright J-5s. The type could also be operated from water, using a single main and two stabilizer floats. The NB-1s were followed by 30 NB-2s, which were similar apart from the powerplant, which differed to allow war-surplus Wright-Hispano E-4 inline engines of 180-hp rating to be used up. The last two NB-1s were retained by Boeing as part of a

US Navy-sponsored aerodynamic research programme into spinning, and with various modifications these two machines were finally designated NB-3 and NB-4. Production of the Model 21 was completed by five aircraft to a Peruvian order.

There followed the Model 40 already mentioned; this led to a number of derivatives to be disussed later, in relation to Boeing's development as an airline as well as an aircraft manufacturer. The next Boeing aircraft was an altogether different concept: the Model 50 was a large twin-engined flying-boat, designed to a US Navy specification for a patrol boat capable of flying nonstop between San Francisco and Hawaii, a distance of some 2,300 miles. Superficially a fairly conventional aircraft, the Model 50 (US Navy PB-1) had a number of unusual features: the two 800-hp Packard 2A-2500 inline engines were located as a push/pull pair in a long nacelle between the wings above the fuselage; the hull had a metal bottom with built-up wooden topsides; the ailerons had aerodynamic balances in the form of

An NB-1 trainer perches on the landing gear favoured in the 1920s, with a single main float and two balancers.

auxiliary surfaces strut-mounted above them, while the rudder and elevators were horn-balanced; and the whole structure was a model of aerodynamic cleanliness compared with contemporary boats. The sole PB-1 was used for a variety of experimental purposes, and in 1928 became the XPB-2 when fitted with a pair of 800-hp Pratt & Whitney Hornet geared radials to allow the propellers to turn more slowly than the engines, and so operate more efficiently. This factor became even more important as better fuels and improved designs allowed engine revolutions to be increased for more power.

The modifications to the Model 21 to make the type spinnable had at the same time introduced a tendency to flat-spin, and this was one of the reasons that Boeing decided to develop with its own funds a new trainer with revised wings using the type of thin aerofoil much favoured by designers during the First World War. This Model 64 first flew in February 1926, and was offered to both the US Army and the US Navy. Neither service accepted the type, and only limited development was undertaken before the prototype was sold to Pacific Air Transport.

Despite the disbelief of its competitors, who fondly imagined that the company had made a bid far too low, Boeing Air Transport and its Boeing Model 40A biplanes were soon bringing home the profits. The airline and the aircraft manufacturer were in legal terms quite separate bodies, but shared a common management team, which made it certain that the airline received the aircraft it needed, and that the airline developed only in such a way that could be served by Boeing aircraft. However, there was no doubting the overall efficiency of the system, as indicated in 1928 by Boeing Air Transport's take-over of Pacific Air Transport, which operated between San Francisco and Seattle. With their operations merged, the two airlines were known as the Boeing System.

Nothing breeds success like success, and Boeing was soon expanding rapidly: early in 1929 Boeing bought the Hamilton Metalplane Company, which continued to operate as a semi-independent unit, and during the summer of the same year Boeing purchased the Hoffar-Breeching Shipyard (located at Vancouver on Canada's western seaboard), which became Boeing Aircraft of Canada Ltd for the local manufacture of American-designed aircraft. More significant by far, however, was the total reorganization of the company along big-business lines: there was established the United Aircraft and Transport Corporation as a holding company for the capital of the Boeing Airplane Company, Boeing Air Transport, Chance Vought Corporation, Hamilton Aero Manufacturing Company, Hamilton Metalplane Company, Pacific Air Transport, and Pratt & Whitney Aircraft Company. All these companies continued to operate within their previously established sectors, but the overall control of the conglomerate ensured that there was no internal

competition or duplication, and that wherever possible each company used the products of another in the group. So it became standard for aircraft originating from the Boeing Airplane Company to have Pratt & Whitney engines and Hamilton propellers unless the buyer specified to the contrary. Further acquisitions at this highly profitable but difficult time were the Sikorsky Aircraft Corporation, the Stearman Aircraft Company and the Standard Steel Propeller Company in the products area; and the National Air Transport, Stout Airlines and Varney Air Lines companies in the transport area. The operations of the airlines were rationalized wherever possible, and though they continued to operate under their original names, they were controlled within the United Aircraft and Transport Corporation by an overall management unit, the United Airlines Inc. William E. Boeing himself headed the Boeing Air

The Model 64 was sold by Pacific Air Transport to Mrs Lyn Healy of Reno, Nevada, who flew it with a J-5 engine.

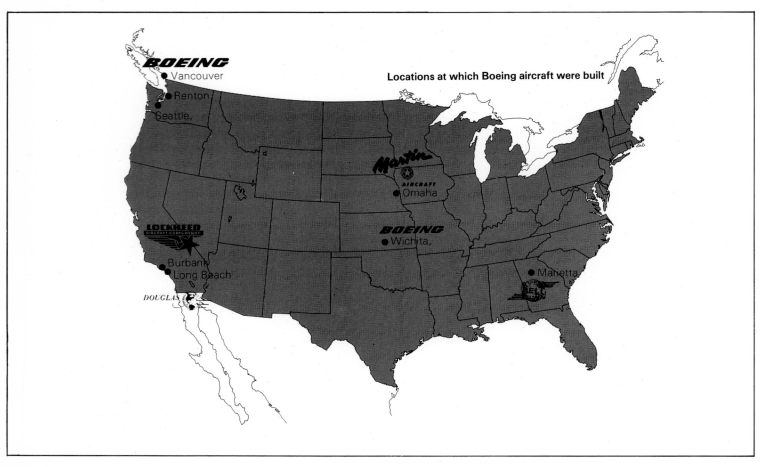

Locations at which Boeing aircraft were built

Transport and Boeing Airplane companies, and was also chairman of the board of the United Aircraft and Transport Corporation, of which Rentschler was president.

Highly cost-effective in this form, UATC was soon in trouble during the terrible days of the depression that followed the Wall Street crash of 1929. In 1934 legislation was passed (notably the Air Mail Act) to ban any one company from owning interests in both the manufacturing of aircraft and the use of aircraft for commercial airline operations. UATC therefore had to divide itself: under the control of a newly-formed United Aircraft Corporation were the Hamilton Standard Propeller Company, Pratt & Whitney, Sikorsky and Vought; the United Air Lines Transport Corporation controlled Boeing Air Transport, National Air Transport, Pacific Air Transport, Stout Airlines and Varney Air Lines; but, oddly enough, the Boeing Airplane Company split off entirely, with Stearman as a wholly-owned subsidiary. William E. Boeing at this time retired from the company.

But while these financial and political wranglings had been taking place, the Boeing Airplane Company had been busily engaged in its true task, the design and construction of aircraft, notably the Model 40A and its successors, to ensure and then build on the success of Boeing Air Transport. At the same time, the proven efficiency of the Model 40A demonstrated that Boeing had finally come of age as a major manufacturer of civil as well as of military aircraft in the USA.

At a time when the airline business was just beginning to open up right across the USA, it was inevitable that operators would soon appreciate how to get the most out of their aircraft by adaptation and modification, and the history of the Model 40A gives major proof of this: for while overall production of Model 40s (excluding the original Model 40 itself) amounted to 80 aircraft, these appeared in no less than nine variants: 25 Model 40As, an uncertain number of Model 40Bs (all conversions from Model 40As and later designated Model 40B-2s), 38 Model 40B-4s, one Model 40B-4A, 10

Model 40Cs, four Model 40H-4s, one Model 40X and one Model 40Y. The Model 40B was a Model 40A retrofitted with the newer 525-hp Pratt & Whitney Hornet radial, which increased performance slightly at the expense of a small reduction in range; the Model 40B-4 was built to carry four passengers on the same Hornet engine as that fitted to the Model 40B/Model 40B-2, mail capacity being reduced to 500 lb; the Model 40B-4A was an engine test-bed aircraft for Pratt & Whitney, originally powered by a 650-hp Hornet driving a large-diameter propeller; the Model 40C in fact preceded the Model 40B-4, and was a derivative of the Model 40A with seating for four passengers; the Model 40H-4 was the Canadian Boeing equivalent of the Model 40B-4; the Model 40X was an executive transport version for the Associated Oil Company with two open cockpits and a cabin for two; and the Model 40Y, like the Model 40X, was an adaptation of the Model 40C and intended for use as an executive transport, in this instance by the Standard Oil Company,

with refinements such as a cowled engine and wheel spats.

As can be seen from the adaptation history of the Model 40 series, Boeing Air Transport and other customers for the type soon found that there was a growing demand for passenger accommodation, and that this could be met in part by cutting back on air-mail capacity. The Boeing Airplane Company in association with Boeing Air Transport soon decided, however, that the growth of airline operations called for a specialized airliner designed principally to carry passengers rather than mail. The result was the Model 80, which could carry 12 passengers over a range of 545 miles on the power of three 410-hp Pratt & Whitney Wasp radials, mounted one on the nose and one each on the inner set of interplane struts. The first Model 80 was flown in August 1928, and licensed on 22 October of the same year. Only four Model 80s were built, but one of these has the distinction of being the first airliner in the world to carry an air stewardess, when Ellen Church worked the sector between

San Francisco and Cheyenne on 15 May 1930.

Even the Model 80 could not meet the steadily increasing demand for airline seats, and Boeing responded with the Model 80A, which could carry 18 passengers in basically the same fuselage thanks to the adoption of three 525-hp Pratt & Whitney Hornet radials. It is interesting to note that freight was by now becoming a significant part of airline economics, and the capacities for the Model 80 and Model 80A are quoted as 1,000 lb and 898 lb respectively. Production of the Model 80A totalled 10 aircraft, which were redesignated Model 80A-1 when fitted with additional vertical tail area. Two aircraft started as Model 80As were not completed as such: the eleventh became the sole Model 226, an expensively finished executive transport for the Standard Oil Company, while the twelfth became the sole Model 80B, with an open cockpit for the two pilots in response to complaints about the 'new' enclosed type of the basic Model 80 series. Airline comparison of the Model 80A and Model 80B soon

The Model 40 failed largely because of its obsolete and heavy Liberty powerplant, later replaced by a radial.

convinced the pilots of the advantages offered by the enclosed cockpit, and the Model 80B was revised to Model 80A-1 standard.

Although Boeing's main efforts were directed towards its airliner series and the new fighter family under development, the company also found time for a number of other projects. These served to display its increasing versatility, and comprised the Model 81 trainer, Model 95 freight/air-mail carrier, Model 203 trainer, Model 6 passenger flying-boat, Model 204 passenger flying-boat, and Steel-Truss Glider.

Though generally unsuccessful, the Model 64 trainer had been considered worthy of development along limited lines, notably the substitution of a wing based on thicker aerofoil sections. From this Boeing evolved the Model 81, with the revolutionary Fairchild-Caminez four-cylinder radial engine. A single Model 81 was bought by the

the original Model 40. This was designed in 1928 as a mail and freight carrier, and continued the classic feature of an open pilot's cockpit located well back along the fuselage behind the payload compartment located on the aircraft's centre of gravity. The first of 25 Model 95s flew on 29 December 1928, and all 25 were was delivered between January and May 1929: 20 to Boeing Air Transport, one to National Air Transport and the remaining four to Western Air Express. It is interesting to note that several Model 95s were subsequently bought by Latin American air forces for conversion into 'bombers'; one Model 95 was modified as a two-seater

with more fuel capacity for experimental long-range flights, and made several nonstop flights across the USA with the aid of inflight-refuelling before crashing. One other Model 95 became the single Model 95A when fitted with a lower-powered version of the Hornet that was used on the standard Model 95s.

The Boeing trainer line took a real step forward with the introduction of the Model 203 in 1929. This was designed to compete with the increasing number of utility and training biplanes of sturdy construction and adequate performance emanating from the drawing boards of companies such as Travel Air and Waco, and the dual

capability of the Model 203 was made possible by the fact that the front cockpit could accommodate one pupil with dual controls, or two passengers. A trim-looking biplane, the Model 203 has the distinction of being the last Seattle-designed aircraft to use a welded steel-tube fuselage. Construction of the Model 203 totalled four, and all were delivered to the Boeing School of Aeronautics. A fifth airframe was completed as the sole production Model 203A, with a 165-hp Wright J-6-

The Model 95 *Boeing Hornet Shuttle* **was used for early experiments in aerial refuelling, a field of effort where Boeing later ruled paramount.**

5 radial replacing the Axelson units of the Model 203s. The four Model 203s were later re-engined to Model 203A standard. After several years of solid service the Model 203As were revised with larger vertical tails, and the fleet was boosted by another two aircraft built at the Boeing School of Aeronautics, one in 1935 and the other in 1936. The life of the seven Model 203As was quite long: three were later modified to Model 203B standard, and the four other aircraft remained in service as primary trainers with the Boeing school until after the USA's entry into the Second World War. The designation Model 203B above applied to three aircraft (the original factory and the two school-built Model 203As) used for more advanced training with extra flight instruments and the installation of 220-hp Lycoming R-680 radials.

The next Boeing design was an incredible throwback: two Model 6Ds and six Model 6Es, which were in design very close to the B-1 flying-boat of 1919. However, the new boats were structurally very different, and had far more modern performance. All eight boats were four-seaters; the two Model 6Ds (which had the alternative designation B-1D) were lighter in

structure than their successors, and were powered by a 220-hp Wright J-5F Whirlwind radial and a 420-hp Pratt & Whitney Wasp respectively, while the six heavier Model 6Es (alternative designation B-1E) were all powered by 410-hp Wasps. The true position of these boats in Boeing's overall scheme is given by the next two aircraft, which started life as Model 6Es but were completed as Model 204s, with seating for five but otherwise very similar to the Model 6Es. The sole Model 204B was a dual-control version of the Model 204, built for William Boeing but later used, in a fashion that indicates the repetitive nature of history, on the Seattle – Victoria air-mail route. The final examples of this basic type were four Model C-204 Thunderbirds built by Canadian Boeing: These were the first aircraft built by this Boeing subsidiary, which went on to evolve the Totem monoplane flying-boat, of which only one example was built. Canadian Boeing's last design was its next: the Steel-Truss Glider, of which a few examples were built.

'The Boeing Bug' trademark, adopted in 1926, stands out strongly in this view of the elegant Model 203, the third of the original four built.

Perhaps the definitive Boeing biplane fighter, the F4B-4 and its US Army equivalent, the P-12E, are remembered with fondness by all who flew or saw them. This F4B-4 was restored in 1961 but unfortunately given the markings of a US Navy squadron, VF-1, which never operated the type. It has since been repainted in the correct livery, that of US Marine Corps squadron VF-9M.

Boeing Air Transport's four Model 80 tri-motors (the first is shown) introduced such novelties as a stewardess, and were later modified to have low-drag ring cowlings on the outer engines.

US Navy for evaluation under the designation XN2B-1, but the engine proved so troublesome that it was replaced by the more powerful Wright J-6-5 radial. Despite the improved performance and serviceability coming from this change, the US Navy ordered no further Model 81s. It had been the second of two airframes that the US Navy had bought, and Boeing persevered with development of the first: realizing the unsuitability of the Fairchild-Caminez powerplant, which was hopelessly unreliable, Boeing switched to the 145-hp Axelson radial to produce the useful if unspectacular Model 81A, which was used by the Boeing School of Aeronautics in California. (A subsidiary of Boeing Air Transport, the flying school was allocated to United Air Lines when the UATC was divided in 1934.) Further alterations to this same aircraft resulted in the designations Model 81B (with 115-hp Axelson radial) and Model 81C (revised vertical tail and 100-hp Kinner K-5 radial).

Of considerably greater importance was the Model 95, a spin-off from

A BRIGHT FUTURE

BY THE LATE 1920s Boeing was recognized as an all-round manufacturer, capable of the design and production of first-class civil and military aircraft. However, the success of the Model 15 fighter and its descendents seems to have found a favoured spot in the company's design department. Improvements that were in themselves small, but all the same important, had kept the PW-9/FB/F2B/F3B series in profitable production, but it was clear that the same basic idea could be reworked to produce a vastly improved fighter type, one that would be of interest yet again to both services and so secure for Boeing very profitable production orders.

The design of the new aircraft, which was entirely a private venture, led to the first flight of the Model 83 on 25 June 1928. It was a decisive moment in Boeing's history, for the Model 83 was the first of no fewer than 586 production derivatives for widespread service with the US and other air forces until the period just before the outbreak of the Second World War. But despite the great things ahead of this prototype, there was little new in the Model 83. Rather than breaking revolutionary new ground, it brought together in just the right blend, all Boeing's previous experience with aerodynamics, structure and powerplant. Boeing had judged its moment nicely: the US forces were still cautious about accepting anything that was entirely new, but were beginning to realize that the limits of the biplane formula accepted without question since the First World War were being reached in the late 1920s. So far as fighters were concerned, the US forces agreed, a new generation was needed to restore the balance that had begun to swing strongly in favour of the high-performance bomber. What they needed, therefore, was a link with the past that would also open the way to the future. With the Model 83 Boeing provided such a link: it combined the virtually standard Pratt & Whitney Wasp radial engine with an airframe that took advantage of all previous experience and lessons to offer a new standard of refinement in the aircraft's basic strength and flight handling, together with greatly improved performance.

Visually, the feature that most easily distinguished the family which came out of the Model 83 from that of the Model 15 was the parallel-chord wing of the later series. However, in construction the wing was almost identical, being based upon a pair of strong mahogany ply/spruce box spars and ribs bandsawed from mahogany three-ply, but with corrugated dural ailerons of semi-monocoque structure. The same type of semi-monocoque structure was used for the tail surfaces. But the construction of the fuselage was new: the forward and central sections were of welded steel tube, while the aft section was bolted up from square-section dural tube. Although a mixed fuselage construction had been used on other types (notably the F2B-1), the direct bolting of tubes to each other by means of dural gussets (rather than through the agency of tabs welded to the longerons) had been pioneered only on the Model 80A. A useful feature of the basic design allowed for an auxiliary fuel tank to be carried under the fuselage. The engine was a 450-hp Pratt & Whitney R-1340 Wasp, initially of a long-nose variety produced to meet objections that the bluff shape of the standard radial spoilt designers' efforts to provide their aircraft with clean entry lines. After early flight tests, this engine was replaced by a standard Wasp, which was considerably cheaper to produce and which reduced speed by very small amounts.

The new fighter appeared in two slightly different prototype forms: the Model 83, which first flew in June 1928, had through-axle type landing gear and was fitted with an arrester hook; the Model 89, which first flew in August 1929, had divided main landing gear units and attachment points under the fuselage for a 500-lb bomb. US Navy evaluation of both types was soon under way, the Model 83 at San Diego, California, and the Model 89 at Anacostia, Maryland. The US Army took the chance to test the Model 89 at Bolling Field, which shared an airfield with Anacostia. Both prototypes were owned by Boeing, but were always mentioned as XF4B-1s in US Navy files.

Flight trials and service tests

proved wholly successful, and the US Navy immediately ordered the type into production as the F4B-1: this production version combined the landing gear and bomb provision of the Model 89 with the arrester hook of the Model 83 in an altered form which Boeing labelled as the Model 99. Both prototypes were altered to this standard before purchase by the US Navy. The initial production contract called for 27 F4B-1s, and these were delivered between June and August 1929. When

delivered, the F4B-1s were fitted with neat fairings behind each of the protruding cylinder heads; but these were soon removed, as it was found that this improved engine cooling and, oddly enough, increased maximum speed slightly. Additionally, one of this initial production batch was converted into a special single-seat transport for the Assistant Secretary of the Navy under the designation F4B-1A. The modifications involved additional fuel tankage, the installation of a cowling ring over the cylinder heads, and the removal of the armament.

Boeing was also aware of some useful export and commercial interest in the type, and produced the Model 100 to meet this demand: four basic Model 100 aircraft (one each for the Bureau of Air Commerce and for Pratt & Whitney, and two for Boeing as demonstration and display aircraft) were preceded by a single Model 100A convertible two-seater for Howard Hughes, who modified the aircraft

This was the last-but-one F4B-3, out of 21 built, and introduced an all-metal fuselage and other refinements.

greatly over a long period.

The US Army also became interested in the fighter, and Boeing received an initial order for 10 Model 102 fighters under the US Army designation P-12. These first aircraft, all delivered in April 1929, were virtually the same as the US Navy's F4B-1s with the exception of the last, which was completed as the sole XP-12A (Model 101) development aircraft. Compared with its companions, the XP-12A featured Frise-type ailerons with their hinge lines parallel to the spars, revised elevators, a long-chord engine cowl, and shorter main landing gear legs. Full testing of the modifications was prevented by the total loss of the aircraft in a mid-air collision shortly after its delivery. Both services were delighted with their new fighters, and orders began to flow in to the Boeing factory. On the US Navy side, the F4B-1 was followed by 46 F4B-2 (Model 233) aircraft equivalent to the US Army's P-12Cs with short-chord ring cowlings, Frise-type ailerons, revised elevators, a spreader-bar landing gear and castoring tailwheel; 21 F4B-3 (Model 235) fighters based on Boeing's Model 218 (XP-925), which introduced a semi-monocoque fuselage; 92 F4B-4 (Model 235) fighters basically similar to the F4B-3s apart from larger vertical tail surfaces and (on the last 45 aircraft) a life raft stowed in the pilot's headrest fairing; and by 23 F4B-4A radio-controlled target aircraft converted from various US Army P-12 models handed over in 1941.

As noted above, the US Army's first version was the P-12, of which 9 were built. These were followed over the years by 90 examples of the P-12B (Model 102B) fighter, in what was at the time the largest such order for the US Army since 1921, this model having the ailerons and elevators pioneered on the XP-12A; 95 examples of the P-12C (Model 222), an improved version of the P-12B with detail modifications, a narrow-chord ring cowling and a spreader-bar landing gear arrangement; 35 examples of the P-12D (Model 227), in fact the last aircraft of the batch ordered as P-12Cs but with minor modifications and 525-hp rather than 450-hp Wasp engines; 110 of the P-12E (Model 234) with the semi-monocoque fuselage and the tail surfaces introduced on the Model 218; and by 25 examples of the P-12F (Model 251), originally part of the P-12E order, with the 500-hp SR-1340E engine developing its rated power at 11,000 ft rather than 7,000 ft. Quite apart from service with US Army 'pursuit' squadrons, the P-12 was also used

extensively for experimental and trials purposes: among these variants were the sole XP-12G, converted from a P-12B by the installation of a turbocharged Y1SR-1340G/H engine; the sole XP-12H, converted from the thirty-third P-12D by the installation of a geared G1SR-1340E engine; the P-12J evolved from a standard P-12E with a 575-hp SR-1340H engine and a special bomb sight; seven YP-12Ks produced by fitting fuel-injected SR-1340E engines to the XP-12E, P-12J and five standard P-12Es; and one XP-12L produced by fitting a YP-12K with a turbocharger of the Type F-7 model.

Production for the US Army and the US Navy was vitally important for Boeing, but the F4B/P-12 basic fighter also proved attractive to a number of export customers, and this extra production was very useful for the company. Many of these export aircraft were modelled closely on variants already

in service with the US forces, but a government ruling against the export of types in service with the US forces meant that Boeing had to devise new model numbers to get round the rule. So the two Model 100E fighters for Siam were in reality all but identical with the US Army's P-12E; 14 Model 256 fighters were delivered to Brazil, and these were diverted from the US Navy's order for F4B-4s; and another nine aircraft were delivered to Brazil under the designation Model 267, this version combining the wings of the P-12E with the fuselage, tail surfaces and landing gear of the F4B-3. In addition to these export versions, Boeing also built a single Model 100F (basically P-12F) for Pratt & Whitney,

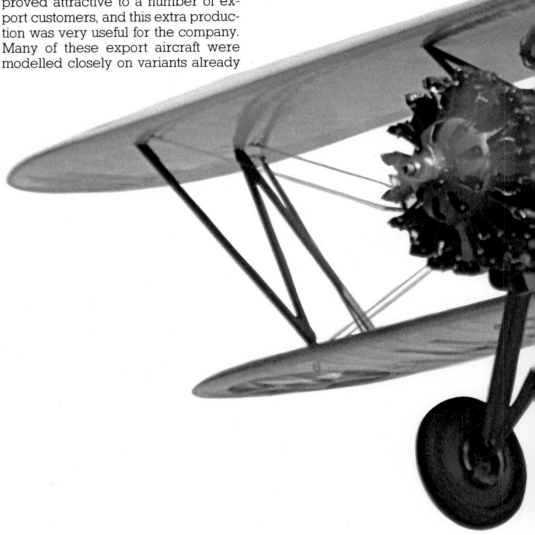

Its serial number (29-354) shows this aircraft to be the second of the US Army's P-12 fighters, all nine of which were delivered in April 1929. The overall feeling of neatness is only slightly spoiled by the uncowled radial and the stalky appearance of the main landing gear.

while one P-12E and two F4B-4s passed into civilian hands.

The importance of the F4B and P-12 series is enormous, not only for the company but for aviation in general. The company profited handsomely and was thus able to go on from strength to strength with the design of more advanced aircraft; for aviation the part played by the F4B and P-12 is harder to pin down, as it is concerned with the basic aircraft's magnificent flight handling and quick manoeuvring. These allowed US Army and US Navy pilots to display their aircraft to the best advantage, both at flying displays and for the photographers of the glossy magazines of the time, so doing much to increase the 'air-mindedness' of the US public with their snappy formations and dazzling colour schemes, based on the use of sharply contrasting tones. Boeing fully realized that one of its main strengths, especially in dealings with the US forces, was its generally cautious approach to design, with only slow introduction of 'radical' features However, it was clear that with the F4B/P-12 series the life of the biplane was nearing its end. Monoplanes were already fairly common in the civil market, and a number of monoplane racers (though often likely to come apart in the air during violent turns, or to come to grief while landing) had provided clear proof of the new levels of performance that

could be achieved by combining this layout with either an inline or a radial engine. So just as production for the F4B/P-12 series was getting into its stride, Boeing launched the design of two basic monoplane types: the Model 96 (US Army XP-9) arose from an official requirement for a monoplane fighter, while the Model 202 and Model 205 were closely related designs of a less radical approach, and came out of the company's feeling that the Model 96 might be too radical, and so present problems that might lead the armed forces to reject the type completely, or to call for solutions that would tie up too much time or money to make it worthwhile.

The Model 96 was much delayed, and first flew only in September 1930. It was a sleek high-wing braced monoplane powered by the 600-hp Curtiss SV-1570 inline. Although maximum speed was 213 mph, performance was generally inferior to that estimated, and control was difficult. No further development was undertaken, but the design of the Model 96 proved of benefit to Boeing, for it introduced to the company the type of semi-monocoque fuselage structure of sheet dural laid over metal formers: such a structure for the rear fuselage appeared next on the Model 200 Monomail and the Model 202/205 fighters.

The basic design used in the Models 202 and 205 had originated

from a Boeing intention to develop a Model 97 from the Model 89 by the removal of the lower wing and the addition of additional struts to support the upper wing, which was also to be moved aft. However, with the decision to move over to all-metal structures, Boeing abandoned the Model 97 in favour of the Models 202 and 205. (The designation numbers between 103 and 199 were reserved for aerofoils designed by Boeing, which explains the sudden jump from the Model 102 to Model 200.) The Model 202 was tested by the US Army under the unofficial designation XP-15, and the Model 205, which differed from the Model 202 only in being fitted as a fighter-bomber for carrier operations, was considered by the US Navy as the XF5B-1. In most aerodynamic respects the Models 202 and 205 were related to the F4B/P-12 type except for the provision of only a single wing and the consequent need for additional strutting, and so suffered in comparison with other fighters of the time in terms of manoeuvrability and climb rate, though speed was improved. Neither was ordered into production, but Boeing was able to incorporate certain structural novelties in the later variants of the F4B/P-12 family.

The last biplane to be designed by Boeing at Seattle was the Model 236, which was produced to meet a continued US Navy requirement for

Above left: **Progress from biplane to monoplane layout was not achieved without problems, and typical of such transition aircraft was the Model 202 with its heavily braced parasol wing.**

Above: **The XF6B was Boeing's last biplane design, and brought together in a single package all the company's experience with this format. But when it appeared in 1933 the design was already obsolete.**

Below: **The new monoplane era was brought in by the pioneering Model 200 mailplane, with its clean lines and retractable landing gear.**

biplane fighters of improved performance but yet able to operate from current aircraft-carriers by virtue of relatively low take-off and landing speeds. The Model 236 was the high point of Boeing's biplane philosophy, and was designed round the 625-hp Pratt & Whitney Twin Wasp Jr radial. Service tests of this clean biplane with sturdy landing gear began in April 1933, under the initial designation XF6B-1, revised in April 1934 to XBFB-1 as a reflection of the type's dual role of fighter and fighter-bomber.

The period before the US Army's request for the XP-9 monoplane fighter may be regarded as the era

that resulted from the First World War: biplane designs built with wood or mixed wood/metal structures. The dividing line is therefore 1929, and from this time onwards Boeing began to display a more innovative streak, in response to a more adventurous tendency in its markets. This is reflected in the Models 97, 202 and 205, but these were in many respects intermediate designs bridging the two eras. Boeing proved itself well suited to the task of adapting to the era of the all-metal monoplane, but it is interesting to note that the change brought about an alteration in Boeing's basic philosophy: in the earlier era the company had been respected as a major manufacturer of fighter aircraft and light transports; in the later era multi-engined heavy bombers and transports became the Boeing hallmark. The situation was not as clear-cut as this at the time, for just as the Models 97, 202 and 205 spanned the design gap between the two eras, aircraft such as the Model 200 bridged the conceptual difference between the two periods.

The Model 200 Monomail may justly be regarded as the true founder of Boeing's new age, and as one of the most important aircraft designs in history. The Model 200 was designed to meet exactly the same need as the Model 40A, and indeed used the same engine as the Model 40B, although in slightly more powerful form as the 575-hp Hornet B. The Model 200 therefore had an additional 50 hp compared with the Model 40B, but a maximum take-off weight increased by 1,925 lb (to 8,000 lb) and maximum speed raised by 21 mph to 158 mph. Wing area was reduced by only 12 sq ft, so this very considerable increase in capability had to result from some revolutionary aerodynamic and/or structural features. These were not hard to spot: the Model 200 was a low-wing cantilever monoplane of all-metal construction with clean lines, a finely-cowled engine and retractable landing gear. In other respects the Model 200 was old-fashioned, or at least conservative in its design approach: the arrangement of the payload compartment and the pilot followed established practice, and additionally still located the pilot in an open cockpit. However, the factor which prevented the Model 200 from an even greater advance over the Model 40B was lack of a controllable-pitch propeller: current propellers, which could be adjusted only on the ground, meant that high performance in the air could only be achieved at the expense of take-off performance, while adequate take-off performance (especially on high air fields) could only be guaranteed if cruising performance was reduced. The Model 200 first flew on 6 May 1930, a date of considerable importance to Boeing and to aviation history, and the sole aircraft was at first used for mail flights on Boeing Air Transport's sector of the transcontinental route.

Just as the original Model 40 had been schemed as a mailplane and then adapted for the carriage of mail and passengers, so too was the design of the Model 200 rapidly adapted to a similar role, the variant being designated Model 221 and named Monomail. The fuselage of the Model 221 was lengthened by 8 in compared with that of the Model 200, but this was sufficient, together with internal re-arrangement, to provide separate compartments for 750 lb of mail and six passengers. This second aircraft first flew on 18 August 1930, and was soon modified to Model 221A standard, with the fuselage lengthened by a further 2 ft 3 in to make possible the accommodation of another two passengers. The original Model 200 was also brought up to Model 221A standard, but production of this crucial type remained just two aircraft – it was clear that passenger capacity was too limited, and that the state of the aeronautical art (largely in propellers) could not match Boeing's aerodynamic dream quite yet.

Boeing's new vision in aerodynamics and structures was also used in the development of two company-funded bomber prototypes, the Model 214 and Model 215. The two aircraft were really scaled-up versions of the Model 200 with twin- rather than single-engined powerplant. And like the Model 200, the Models 214 and 215 matched established internal arrangements and open cockpits with the new monoplane layout and retract-

able landing gear. Two unusual features were the tandem cockpits for the pilot and co-pilot, made necessary by the extreme slimness of the fuselage, and the use of servo tabs for the first time on an American aircraft, to help reduce the pilots' control forces. The two aircraft differed initially only in the powerplant fitted: the Model 214 had a pair of 600-hp Curtiss GIV-1570 inlines, while the Model 215 featured two 575-hp Pratt & Whitney R-1860-13 Hornet radials.

The Model 215 was completed first, and made its initial flight in the hands of Les Tower, one of Boeing's great test pilots, on 13 April 1931. Though the property of Boeing, the Model 215 was tested at Wright Field under the designation XB-901; when bought by the US Army later in 1931 it became the YB-9, and official enthusiasm for the type convinced the company that large-scale production orders would soon flood in. However, the YB-9 suf-

fered for being a pioneer in the field, for the Martin XB-907 that appeared slightly later was a more advanced aircraft and so entered production instead of the YB-9.

The Model 214 was still incomplete when the US Army bought it, together with the XB-901, in August 1931. De-

signated Y1B-9, this inline-engined type was first flown on 5 November 1931, and was soon converted to a powerplant identical with that of the YB-9. Though no large production orders were envisaged by the US Army, the service appreciated that much operational experience could be gained with the basic type, so it ordered a pre-production batch of five Y1B-9As, which Boeing produced under the designation Model 246. The vertical tail surfaces were altered, and many internal modifications, in both equipment and structure, were added. The powerplant consisted of two 600-hp Y1G1SR-1860B Hornet radials, and military load was made up of two 0.30-in machine-guns and four 600-lb bombs. Delivery of the five aircraft was made between July 1932 and March 1933, and in service they played an important but unglamorous role in helping the US Army to develop its multi-engined bomber techniques.

The Model 200/221 and the Model 214/215/246 were milestones in the growth of civil and military aviation respectively. But where they failed was in not going far enough into the future: they were first-generation aircraft, still using the old pattern of internal arrangement, and hampered by

the absence of items of auxiliary equipment that would have allowed them to develop their true potential. This lesson was forcibly brought home to Boeing by Martin's receipt of the bomber production order the Seattle company thought was theirs. The company determined not to make the same mistake with the latest aircraft taking shape on the drawing-board. This was the Model 247, another classic design and the true ancestor of the twin-engined modern airliner. Boeing designers used their experience with the earlier metal aircraft to produce a clean low-wing monoplane of all-metal stressed-skin construction, again with two radial engines and retractable landing gear, but this time with enclosed accommodation for the pilots as well as the passengers. The Model 247 was designed to replace the various tri-motors in wide service with the US airlines, with the distinct advantages of being able to climb with one engine stopped, even when fully loaded, and of having a maximum speed some 60 mph greater than the tri-motors. It was obvious right from the start that if the Model 247 met its requirement, it would offer very important operating advantages over its competitors. The four most important

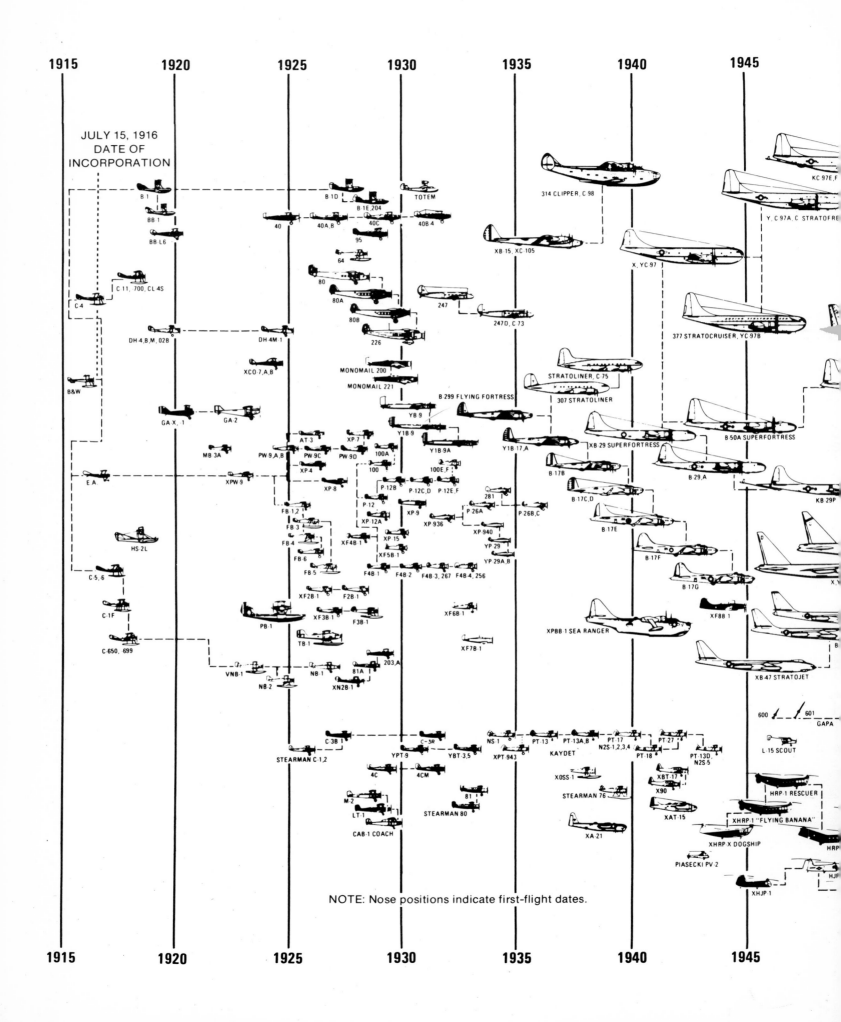

NOTE: Nose positions indicate first-flight dates.

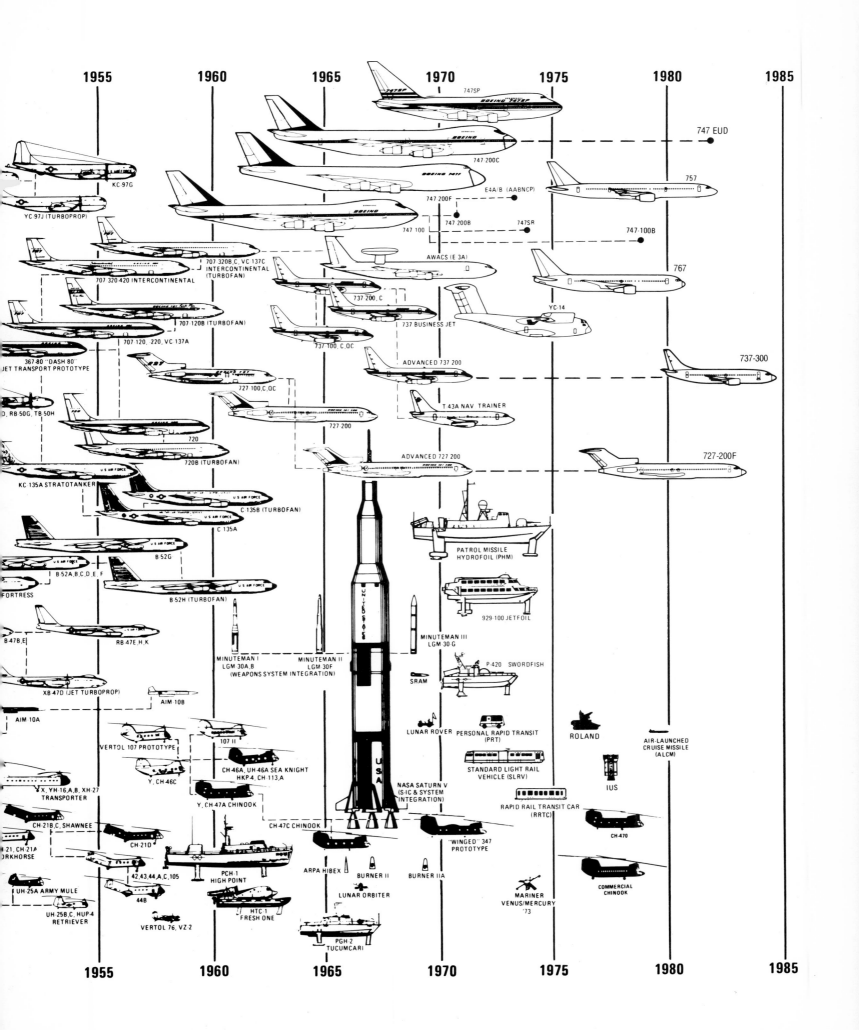

factors acting against the success of the design were the limited capacity of the passenger cabin (only 14 persons), the obstruction of the cabin by the wing spars, the lack of trailing-edge flaps, and the lack of variable-pitch propellers.

Nevertheless, the design clearly had great promise, and the airlines of the United Air Lines, Inc ordered 70 Model 247s in 1932. However, they opted for the 525-hp Wasp in place of the 700-hp Hornet proposed by Boeing, and this reduced passenger capacity to 10. The first Model 247 flew on 8 February 1933, and the type entered service on 30 March of the same year. Within three months United could field no fewer than 30 of the type, which immediately set about breaking most US air transport records, including the lopping of no

less than 7 hours off the coast-to-coast transcontinental record with a time of 19 hours 45 minutes.

The Model 247's worst operational failing, one compounded by the lack of flaps, was poor take-off and landing performance on high-altitude air-fields. This was partially the result of the low-powered engines chosen by UAL, but partially because the ground-adjustable propellers were normally set to provide cruising efficiency, which was where profit was made. This fault was remedied by the introduction of the Model 247D, which introduced Hamilton-Standard controllable-pitch propellers, drag-reducing NACA cowlings for the engines, and windscreens that sloped backwards rather than forwards. Only 61 Model 247s were completed as such (two going to the German air-

line, Luft Hansa) before production switched to the Model 247D, of which 13 were built. All the Model 247s, with the exception of the two German examples, were later modified to Model 247D standard, though some retained windscreens of the original pattern. Production of the series totalled 75, the missing aircraft being the thirtieth Model 247, which was completed as the sole Model 247A executive transport and flying test-bed for Pratt & Whitney. The Model 247 series did finally make money for Boeing, but the company again lost out on larger orders because of the arrival of a slightly later, and so considerably more versatile, aircraft in the form of the superlative Douglas DC series. In 1942 27 of the surviving Model 247s were impressed for service with the US Army, which designated them C-

Above: Like many other designs from Boeing, the Model 247 was a true pioneer, in this instance of the 'modern' twin-engine airliner, based on stressed-skin construction, clean lines, monoplane layout and retractable landing gear. The example depicted belongs to the Pacific Northwest Aviation Historical Foundation in Seattle. It was built as a Model 247 for United Air Lines, and was later modified to Model 247D standard. It is still airworthy.

Left: One of the main problems with the Model 247 series was lack of capacity, a relatively cramped cabin and the fact that the wing spars passed through the passenger accommodation (visible as the obstruction in the narrow aisle). But the Model 247 was a great 'plane.

73s until they were returned to civil ownership in 1944.

Boeing's next design, the Model 248, appeared to be a backward step. Originating from a combination of Boeing's design experience with fighters together with new structural methods and the US Army's interest in a monoplane fighter, the Model 248 was a radial-engined low-wing monoplane of metal construction. So far so good: but the thin wings were not cantilever structures, and so required external bracing; and the landing gear was of the fixed rather than retractable type. But the design was the result of careful consideration, for Boeing had worked out that such a configuration produced good strength for relatively low drag and weight, so ensuring a general improvement in performance. The braced wing was lighter than a cantilever type, and the bracing wires produced little drag; at the same time, the fixed landing gear was lighter and less complex than a comparable retractable type, and also provided the right anchorage points for the flying wires. The basic correctness of Boeing's thinking is proved by an assessment of the Model 248 in comparison with the Model 251 (P-12F): evaluated by the US Army as XP-936s, the two flying Model 248s had only 22 hp more than the P-12F in terms of available power and were 40 lb heavier, but were 27 mph faster in level flight and possessed a climb rate improved by no less than 475 ft per minute. Impressed, the US Army bought the two aircraft (the third was reserved for static testing) under the designation XP-26, later changed to Y1P-26 and finally to P-26 when the type was

This Model 247D was completed with extra fuel tanks for the 1934 'MacRobertson' air race from the UK to Australia.

ordered into production.

The first XP-936 had flown in April 1932, only four months after the start of prototype construction; initial US Army procurement of P-26A production aircraft was 111, and the first of these, produced under the Boeing designation Model 266, was handed over in January 1934. The only appreciable outside difference between the Model 248 and Model 266 was the revised outline of the latter's wheel

This Model 247D was used by the RAF in the Second World War for research into automatic landing systems.

'pants', which did not extend aft of the landing gear strut. Inside a number of modifications had been made, and soon after delivery the aircraft were modified with a taller headrest to protect the pilot in the event of the aircraft turning over on landing. Interestingly enough, the price received by Boeing for each P-26A was $198 less than that for each of the P-12E variant, which was built in very nearly the same numbers.

From the beginning of the programme, Boeing had been aware that one of the major penalties of a monoplane configuration was a higher wing

loading, and thus a higher landing speed. In an effort to improve on this factor, the company had tested plain flaps on a P-26A, with encouraging results. Such flaps were retrofitted to all the P-26As in service, and all aircraft still in production had them installed at that stage. Despite the importance of the P-26A in American aviation history, as the US Army Air Corps' first all-metal and first monoplane fighter, the type was built in relatively small numbers and in few variant forms, and this shows that the USAAC and Boeing realized that the P-26 series could only be a mid-way

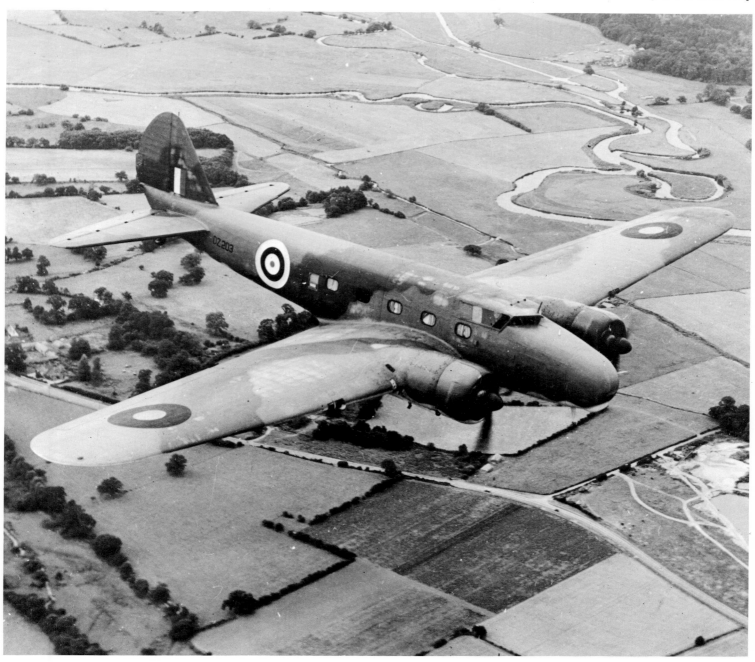

type pending the development of cantilever monoplane fighters with considerably more powerful engines.

Soon after delivery of P-26A aircraft began, the USAAC had increased its order by an additional 25 aircraft, and two of these, under the Boeing designation Model 266A, were completed as P-26Bs with the SR-1340-33 fuel-injected version of the Wasp engine. The two aircraft were delivered in June 1934, and service trials proved so successful in a long evaluation programme that during 1936 all 23 P-26Cs were converted to this standard. These aircraft, the balance of the extra order for 25 aircraft, had been delivered between February and March 1936, and differed from the P-26A only in minor details of fuel supply and carburetion. The Boeing designation for the P-26C was unaltered from that of the P-26A.

Exports of the P-26 series totalled 12 (one to Spain and 11 to China), and these were built under the company designation Model 281, with only minor equipment details marking them apart from the P-26A. It should be noted that the trailing-edge flaps retrofitted to the P-26As were in reality developed for the Model 281, Boeing having felt that while the USAAC could cope with high landing speeds on its well-prepared airfields, the smaller and less sophisticated airfields of China called for a reduced approach and touch-down speed.

The Boeing monoplane fighter concept was taken a stage further with a pair of more advanced fighters, the Model 273 evaluated as the US Navy XF7B-1 and the Model 264 tested by the USAAC under the initial designation XP-940. Despite its later model number, the US Navy type in fact appeared first, for it was in direct response to a 1932 naval requirement

that Boeing started work on the type. Though limited to a single example, the Model 273 is another landmark in US aviation history, for it was the first monoplane fighter to be evaluated by the US Navy when accepted for trials after its first flight on 14 September 1933. Although the powerplant was still the legendary Wasp radial (in a form developing some 50 hp less than that available in the P-26 series), the Model 273 had new features such as cantilever wings, a fully retractable landing gear, enclosed cockpit and (for the first time on a Boeing aircraft) flaps and provision for a controllable-pitch propeller. Compared with the US Navy's standard biplanes, however, the Model 273 was judged to have too high a landing speed and too low a level of aerial agility; on the credit side was a maximum speed of 233 mph, only marginally less than that of the more powerful P-26 series.

The Model 264 was in all respects but service equipment similar to the Model 273, but was built as a private venture by Boeing with active support from the USAAC. Three aircraft were built: the first was tested under the initial designation XP-940, but its cramped cockpit transparency proved troublesome and it was revised with an open cockpit and the new designation YP-29A once it had been bought by the US Army; the second was bought by the military while still under construction, and was completed as the YP-29 with a much roomier cockpit enclosure giving the pilot greater freedom of movement and fields of vision; and the third was finished as the YP-29B with an open cockpit. None of the variants was judged suitable for large-scale production, so the three aircraft were used largely for experimental purposes at various US Army facilities.

Commonly known as the 'Peashooter', the P-26C was built only in small quantities, but formed an effective bridge between the biplane and monoplane eras in the mid-1930s.

If any one thing symbolizes Boeing's contribution to Allied victory in the Second World War, it is the B-17 Flying Fortress that tore the heart out of Germany's industries and transport systems in the hands of the mighty 8th Air Force. Here an example of the final production series, a B-17G with a chin turret, waits to be bombed up on an English airfield.

FROM STRENGTH TO STRENGTH

AFTER ITS CAUTIOUS START with monoplanes, of which only the Model 247 and Model 266 may be considered successful (and then only partially so), Boeing changed its ideas enormously. Gone were the small- and intermediate-size monoplanes of the transition phase from biplane to monoplane configuration, in their place came a huge four-engined aircraft that was, at the time of its first flight on 15 October 1937, the largest aircraft (and also the heaviest) to have been built in the United States up to that time. This was the Model 294, which spanned an impressive 149 ft compared with 80 ft for the Model 80, the next largest Boeing aircraft of Seattle design.

The origins of this monster lay with a 1934 US Army requirement for a truly long-range aircraft suitable for the defence of the USA from bases within that country's mainland: this meant that the Experimental Bomber, Long Range-1 (XBLR-1) had to be capable of striking at targets well out into, or even across, the Atlantic and Pacific Oceans, a requirement that called for a considerable offensive load to be carried over

trans-oceanic ranges. In 1936 the Model 294 was redesignated XB-15. Despite the old-fashioned constructional feature of fabric covering for the wing aft of the main spar, the Model 294 introduced a number of interesting features: a flight engineer to relieve the two pilots of the work involved in the management and control of the four-engined powerplant; cooking and rest facilities for the crew; electrical power provided by a pair of special petrol engines; and a crawlway into the wings behind the engines to permit inflight adjustments of the engines. As the Model 294 was planned, the powerplant was to have comprised a quartet of Allison V-1710 inlines for a total of some 4,600 hp; these were replaced during the construction phase by a similar number of Pratt & Whitney R-1830 Twin Wasp radials for a total of 4,000 hp, and it was clear right from the first flight, in the hands of Boeing's celebrated test pilot Eddie Allen, that the XB-15 was seriously underpowered. The real problem was that engine development had not made such rapid ad-

A bomber ahead of its time, the XB-15 failed because no suitably powerful engines were available in the mid-1930s.

vances as aircraft development in the mid-1930s, and a powerplant of sufficient output for so massive an aircraft just was not available. The fact had been realized by the USAAC fairly early in the XB-15's development, and procurement plans were modified to produce an effective bomber using engines each developing about 1,000 hp. Orders for two more advanced pre-production Y1B-20 models were cancelled, and the XB-15 was used solely for experimental purposes until the Second World War, when the aircraft was pressed into service as a transport under the designation XC-105.

Even as the Model 294 was taking shape in Boeing's experimental shop, the company's most famous aircraft was overtaking it. This was the Model 299, the design of which had been started on 18 June 1934 and which made its first flight on 28 July 1935 under the control of Les Tower. The

Model 299 is better known to history as the B-17 Flying Fortress, of which some 12,731 were built by Boeing and its production associates in the massive Second World War programme, Douglas and Lockheed.

The origins of the Model 299, like those of the Model 294, lay with a USAAC requirement, in this instance one issued in May 1934 and calling for a multi-engined bomber capable of carrying 2,000 lb of bombs over a range of 1,020 miles at 200 mph (but preferably of carrying the same bomb load over a range of 2,200 miles at 250 mph). The schedule envisaged by the USAAC called for the delivery of a prototype for service testing within 16 months, an incredibly short time and one that Boeing could meet only because the company was already working towards such an aircraft. With the Model 294 well along the design road, and the Model 247 already in service, it was hardly surprising that the Model 299 used features of both aircraft. In size it was about mid-way between them; in construction it was closely related to the Model 247; and in con-

figuration it was akin to the Model 294. Where the Model 299 was totally new was in concept: to the USAAC and to American aircraft manufacturers, 'multi-engine' configuration at that time meant two-engined, and while the four-engined layout was not unknown, it had previously been used only as a way to get large aircraft into the air, and not to provide high performance and long range. Boeing's farsightedness was in seeing that it could produce a machine that would handsomely exceed the USAAC's payload/range/speed requirements by the use of four high-powered engines. Some indication of Boeing's success can be gained from a simple comparison with the Douglas DB-1, which came closest to the Model 299 in the evaluation phase of USAAC testing: the Model 299 spanned only 8 ft 3 in more than the Douglas design, was capable of carrying a bomb load of 4,800 lb compared with 2,532 lb, had a maximum speed of 236 mph compared with 220 mph, and could fly substantially farther. The Model 299 was powered by four 750-hp R-1690-E Hornet radials and car-

ried a defensive armament of five 0.30-in machine-guns, while the DB-1 had two 850-hp Wright R-1820-G5 radials and three 0.30-in machine-guns. Despite the relative unit costs of $99,620 and $58,500, the USAAC had little hesitation in opting for the more expensive but initially more capable Model 299. Inter-service rivalry and general shortage of fundings meant that initial purchases had to be small, but the USAAC appreciated that much development work, both technical and operational, could be undertaken, and that the basic design was full of military potential at a time of increasing world unease.

The Model 299 project was a make-or-break affair for Boeing: as the Model 247 and Model 266 had proved to be only marginally profitable, and other projects of the time had come to nothing, the company found itself with a large and highly skilled work force which had almost nothing to do. But rather than lay off large numbers of its employees, the company decided to keep everyone on, though only half the employees worked at any one time. This meant that while all worked two weeks on and two weeks off, one of the company's main assets was kept in being for the day that a major project received large orders. All the personnel's faith had been pinned on the Model 299, and it was something of a disappointment when no great orders were placed immediately after the end of the service test period. But it was realized that economics and US isolationism were the main reasons, and that a rapidly worsening world situation could only mean larger orders if the company could survive until then. And other projects, including a civil transport based on the Model 299, were in the pipeline as extra incentives to stay in readiness for expansion.

Boeing patented the name Flying Fortress for the type after initial Press enthusiasm for its powerful offensive and defensive provisions, only the second time a Boeing aircraft had

been named. Press publicity was even stronger after the Model 299's delivery flight from Seattle to Wright Field, a 2,100-mile nonstop flight across the country at the sensational average speed of 252 mph. The prototype had been privately funded by Boeing, and so had no official US Army designation. Evaluation by the military was not delayed by this, but the prototype Model 299 was unfortunately lost on 30 October 1935, only 10 weeks after delivery, when a US Army pilot tried to take-off with the controls locked. During its brief test period the Model 299 had impressed all with its capabilities (although some were less than enthusiastic about its cost and complexity) and in January 1936 a pre-production batch of 13 YB-17 (later Y1B-17) bombers was ordered, the company designating this revised aircraft with Wright SGR-1820-39 Cyclone radials as the Model 299B. The 12 flying Y1B-17s were delivered between January and August 1937, and formed the equipment of the 2nd Bombardment Group, located at Langley Field. This unit pioneered the operational techniques of heavy bombing, and in this

way fully tested the aircraft's revised internal arrangements and armament (crew reduced from eight to six, and armament increased to 8,000 lb of bombs and five 0.50-in machine-guns). The thirteenth Y1B-17 had been kept back for static testing, but after one of the 2nd Bombardment Group's aircraft flew through a heavy thunderstorm without damage, it was decided that the Model 299's structural strength needed no further proof. The thirteenth aircraft was therefore completed as the sole Y1B-17A with GR-1820-51 radials fitted with Moss/General Electric turbochargers. These engines could thus deliver 800 hp at 25,000 ft, while the standard R-1820-39s of the Y1B-17s were rated at 775 hp at 14,000 ft. The chief tactical advantage of such a powerplant was that the Y1B-17A could reach 295 mph at 25,000 ft compared with the Y1B-17's 256 mph at 14,000 ft. The Y1B-17A had a maximum speed of 311 mph and a service ceiling of more than 30,000 ft, and it was decided to provide a turbocharged powerplant on all future B-17 models.

With the end of the 2nd Bombard-

ment Group's service test period the aircraft were designated plain B-17, and an initial production contract for 39 B-17Bs (Model 299M) was placed during 1938. So started an enormous production programme that falls beyond the scope of this book, though details of the B-17 variants and their construction appear in the display panels on pages 68-69. In summary it may be said that although the B-17's combat debut was inauspicious (20 B-17Cs being supplied as Fortress Is to the RAF, which used them against heavily defended targets and so suffered heavy losses), the type soon proved itself beautifully suited for long-range maritime patrol bombing (the role for which it had been designed). Combat experience proved the need for major equipment improvement (defensive armament, armour, fuel tank protection and high-altitude gear), but once these had been provided the B-17 went from strength to strength. The Flying Fortress played a key part in the Pacific War, but is best remembered as the bomber mainstay of the US 8th Air Force operating in massed daylight

Below: A newly-built B-17G lifts off for a trial flight, the airfield seemingly littered with other aircraft.

Above: The B-17 fleets were the scourge of German industry with precision attacks from high altitude.

raids from bases in England. Here the B-17E soon gave way to the B-17F with additional armament, and finally to the definitive B-17G with powerful nose-mounted armament to deter head-on attacks by German fighters. Boeing's last B-17 was delivered on 13 April 1945, and within months of the war's end most of the many thousands of B-17s had been declared surplus to requirements, though the type did soldier on in a number of special-purpose and experimental roles.

As already noted, the Model 299 had been a make-or-break proposition for Boeing, for the company appreciated that the chances of the USAAC ordering the type before seeing ample proof of its capabilitites were small. Thus Boeing had sounded out the USAAC almost secretly about the likely response to factors such as the four-engined powerplant. Only when the company was fairly certain of favourable response to its basic proposals did it allow the use of a size-able proportion of its limited capital on the construction of so costly and so risky a prototype. However, Boeing's faith in its product was more than justified by the enormous production orders for the B-17, which was exceeded in numbers amongst US bombers only by the Consolidated B-24 Liberator, and in the wide range of the manufacturing process only by another Boeing product, the B-29 Super-fortress, during the Second World War.

Boeing had been able to make do with small-scale production facilities up to and including the Model 247, but it was clear that if the Model 299 proved successful, considerably larger production area would be needed. In 1936, therefore, Boeing began work on the new No. 2 Plant on the riverside frontage of Boeing Field. The site was carefully selected with a view to future development, a far-sighted decision in view of the enormous expansion of B-17 production during the Second World War. In fact the first type to be assembled in the No. 2 Plant was the Model 294, which had been built at the No. 1 Plant, while production of all Boeing aircraft of the later 1930s and 1940s, starting with the 13 examples of the Y1B-17,

Left: A US Navy crewman winds up the inertia starter for the Continental R-670 radial of this N2S-2, basically identical with the USAAF's PT-17.

Below left: The chin turret of the B-17G packed a powerful punch, but experienced German pilots still sliced in with their heavy cannon.

Right: Compared with the B-17E, the B-17F introduced extra fuel and self-sealing oil tanks, and had more guns in an effort to combat German fighters.

Below: Individual guns were not enough to drive off German fighters, so the Fortresses were operated in boxes for overlapping cones of protective fire.

were built at the No. 2 Plant. The only exceptions to this rule were the Model 314 flying-boats and various experimental aircraft, while production of established Boeing types was also spread to other sites. For example, in April 1939 the Boeing subsidiary in Wichita, Kansas ceased to be the Stearman Aircraft Company when it was brought in closer to the main company as the Wichita Division of the Boeing Aircraft Company, though it continued to design and build aircraft under its own designation (mostly trainers of various kinds, notably the great and much-loved Model 75 often known as the Kaydet). When it was seen how large the programme for the B-29 would have to be, the US Government built a new factory at Wichita, and this became the Wichita Division's Plant 2, the original Stearman facility becoming Plant 1. In the event the B-29 was also built at Renton, where the US

Navy had built for Boeing a large production facility for the PBB-1 Sea Ranger; however, with the cancellation of production plans for this massive flying-boat, the US Navy transferred the factory to the US Army for increased B-29 production. The original Boeing company had meanwhile become the Seattle Division of the Boeing Aircraft Company, and in this form grew rapidly within Seattle and neighbouring towns for the manufacture of sub-assemblies and for training and storage. The Seattle Division's growth can be gauged from the fact that the number of employees jumped from 1,755 in January 1938 to 2,960 in December 1938 (with B-17 and Model 307 production in progress), to 8,724 in August 1940, to 28,840 in early 1942, and to a wartime high of 44,754 in January 1945.

Canadian Boeing had started production at a new factory in Vancouver,

British Columbia during the late 1930s, and this first built Blackburn Sharks under licence. In the period between 1937 and 1946 Boeing and its subsidiaries built its own aircraft as well as other companies' designs, while production of Boeing designs was also extended to other manufacturers. For example, at Seattle Boeing built 380 Douglas DB-7 attack bombers, at Wichita 750 Waco CG-4A assault gliders and at Vancouver 362 assorted Consolidated flying-boats; on the other side of the coin Douglas produced 2,995 B-17s at Long Beach, California; Lockheed 2,750 B-17s at its Vega subsidiary located at Burbank, California; Bell 668 B-29s at Marietta, Georgia; and Martin 536 B-29s at Omaha, Nebraska.

Though the main stream of Boeing aircraft had come from the boards of designers located in Seattle, some notable types came from Wichita, as

Stearman or Boeing (Wichita Division) designs. The most famous of these, and one of the great aircraft to appear in the USA between the two world wars, was the Stearman Model 75, a classic biplane trainer. Most of the 8,584 built in the overall Model 70 to Model 76 series (components for another 1,762 were made as spares for the complete aircraft) were produced after Stearman had become the Wichita Division, but the original name stuck, and is still used generally instead of the more correct Boeing Wichita name. Another name that has attached itself strongly to the type is Kaydet, though this name was properly applied only in Canada. Aircraft of the series were built for the USAAC and US Army Air Forces under the designations PT-13, PT-17, PT-18 and PT-27, and for the US Navy under the designations NS and N2S. With the end of the Second World War the

need for these sturdy biplanes disappeared, and many thousands were dumped onto the civil market. Some proof of the type's popularity is given by the fact that in 1950 about 4,125 were on the US civil register, and in 1959 about 2,025 were still in civil service, mostly as crop dusters.

The Wichita designers tried to produce a worthy successor to the biplane series with the Model X-90 and Model X-91, which shared a common airframe. Engined with a 225-hp Lycoming R-680 radial the Model X-90 was intended as a primary trainer, and with a 400-hp Pratt & Whitney R-985 radial the Model X-91 was proposed as a basic trainer. Designed in 1940, the Models X-90/-91 were based on a clean low-wing monoplane layout with fixed tailwheel landing gear and a long glasshouse canopy, built largely of wood, plywood and steel tube to avoid the need for aluminium alloys,

which it was believed would become scarce in any war. But though the sole example built was delivered to the USAAF for testing as the XBT-17 with a Pratt & Whitney engine in January 1942, the shortage of aluminium alloys was avoided, and the service decided to stay with its traditional types.

Wichita's two other designs of the period were the Model X-100 twin-engined prototype for the proposed A-21 attack monoplane, and the Model X-120 twin-engined prototype for the proposed AT-15 Crewmaker bomber trainer. Both were interesting machines, but shared the Model X-91's inability to win a production order.

But all this mighty production effort was in the future when Boeing inau-

Civil counterpart of the Flying Fortress, the Model 307 Stratoliner introduced cabin pressurization, allowing operations above the weather.

The Boeing Model 314A was the greatest civil flying-boat ever built, and the type opened the first economically sensible air services across the Pacific and North Atlantic, combining reliability, safety, comfort and performance.

gurated the No. 2 Plant across the main Seattle-Tacoma road from Boeing Field in 1936. Much still depended on the success or failure of the Model 299, though the company was hoping to halve its losses (or double its success) by producing in parallel with the military Model 299 a civil Model 307. This retained the wings, tail, powerplant and landing gear of the Model 299H (B-17C), which were added to a completely new, advanced fuselage of large-diameter circular section. The reason for this was Boeing's decision to pioneer a major pressurized airliner,

able to cruise at 20,000 ft, where it would avoid some 90 per cent of the adverse weather conditions that troubled less advanced airliners that had to operate in the region of 12,000 ft. The Model 307 was given the special name Stratoliner to indicate its unique asset. Design began in 1935, in parallel with that of the Model 299, but Boeing only began production when it received its first firm order for the type: four examples designated S-307 for Pan American Airways, soon boosted by orders for five SA-307Bs for Transcontinental and Western Air, and for one SB-307B for Howard Hughes. The first Model 307 flew on

the last day of 1938, but was later lost while being flown by the pilot of a would-be buyer. Further trials with later examples confirmed the suspicion that the vertical tail derived from the Model 299H was not up to the job, and Boeing swiftly designed and introduced a new unit that became the hallmark of future piston-engined Boeing aircraft. Production amounted to only these 10 aircraft. During the Second World War Pan American's three Stratoliners were operated by the airline as military transports while retaining their civil registrations, and TWA's five aircraft were taken over by the US Army Air Transport Command as C-75s, though they were still operated by TWA crews. In military service the Model 307s performed with great reliability, carrying VIP passengers mainly over the North and South Atlantic routes.

Pan American was also the starting point for Boeing's 'next' civil aircraft, the Model 314 flying-boat. This had started life before the Model 307, in fact, but it was only when Pan American accepted Boeing's suggested design in 1936 that a proper designation was allocated. Perhaps the greatest civil flying-boat ever produced, the Model 314 became known as the Clipper after Pan American's copyrighted prefix for all its aircraft names, and was based on the wing of the Model 294 bomber with larger engines and a special hull balanced on the water by sponsons rather than by underwing floats. As designed, the Model 314 had only a single vertical tail surface: this was not enough, and was replaced by twin endplate units of oval shape; and finally the central fin was restored as the endplates also turned out to be insufficient on their

Ultimate expression of the B-29 concept, the post-war B-50D offered powerful offensive and defensive armament, radar bombing accuracy and great range, the last as a result of the underwing auxiliary tanks outboard of the engines.

Top: **B-29 fleets based in the Marianas islands burned the heart out of Japan during 1945 with devastatingly effective incendiary raids at low level.**

own. The first Model 314 took to the air on 7 June 1938, and this type was the last to be built at the No. 1 Plant. Pan American's initial order was for six aircraft for use on the airline's trans-Atlantic and trans-Pacific routes, but the total was later raised to 12 by an order for six Model 314As with 1,600-hp rather than 1,200-hp Wright GR-2600 Double Cyclone engines, and fuel capacity increased to boost range from 3,500 miles to 4,200 miles. The Model 314A first flew in March 1940, and all six boats had been handed over by the middle of January 1942. The Model 314s were also improved to Model 314A standard. Pan American did not long enjoy the commercial

advantages of its classic boats: four were taken over by the US Army under the designation C-98, three later being handed over to the US Navy as B-314s to join two acquired directly by the latter, also as B-314s. Another three Clippers were sold to the British Overseas Airways Corporation for the British part of the North Atlantic route.

By the late 1930s it was clear that war in Europe could not long be delayed, and further-sighted Americans saw that there was a good chance that their country too could become tangled in the war. This placed greater emphasis on the development of military rather than civil aircraft,

for even if the USA stayed neutral, her forces needed to be strengthened sufficiently to protect the USA's neutrality. Amongst the country's most urgent needs were two that appealed strongly to Boeing, which now had great of experience with long-range heavy aircraft and with flying-boats: these were a long-range heavy bomber capable of striking at the USA's overseas enemies, and a long-range patrol bomber flying-boat able to detect and attack hostile naval forces making for American shores. In many respects these two requirements may be considered the follow-ups to the XBLR-1/XB-15 specification, now at last made practical by the

The B-29 Superfortress was a dream aircraft, with payload and performance ensured by powerful engines and very clean lines.

Another of the keys to the B-29's performance, especially at high altitude, was the provision of two turbochargers to force air into each of the R-3350 radials.

development of suitably powerful engines and other advances in aviation technology.

Boeing's answer to the two needs were the Model 344 flying-boat and the Model 345 bomber. Despite its later designation number, the Model 345 was in fact the earlier of the two aircraft, starting life as a series of preliminary designs reflecting the USAAC's 1938 request for a study of a pressurized version of the B-17 with tricycle landing gear. This received the Boeing designation Model 334, and design went ahead slowly at company expense, the USAAC having too little money to divert any for the project. However, the progress of German aggression in Europe finally persuaded the release of more funding for military hardware, and on 5 February 1940 the USAAC issued its requirement for a 'Hemisphere Defense Weapon' capable of flying 5,333 miles at a speed of 400 mph with 2,000 lb of bombs to be dropped at the mid-point. Several companies tendered to the specification, but Boeing was well ahead of its competitors and could offer a better aircraft with faster initial deliveries. Boeing's definitive proposal was the Model 345, of which two XB-29 prototypes were ordered on 24 August 1940. A third prototype was later added to the order. Even before the first prototype flew in the hands of Eddie Allen on 21 September 1942, production of the B-29 had been ordered: 250 aircraft were contracted in May 1941, to be built at the Boeing-operated government plant at Wichita; a further 250 were added in January 1942; and by the time of the first XB-29's maiden flight, orders for the B-29 exceeded 1,500, the US Army having brought Bell (Marietta, Georgia), North American (Kansas City, Kansas) and the Fisher Body Divison of General Motors (Cleveland, Ohio) into a major co-production programme.

Construction of the three prototypes was pushed ahead with all speed at the No. 1 Plant in Seattle, and then the parts moved by truck to Boeing

The B-50 development of the B-29 was largely distinguishable by the totally different nacelles for the R-4360 radials. This example is on show at the USAF Museum at Dayton, Ohio.

Field for assembly and initial flight tests. These went ahead smoothly, despite the loss of the second aircraft as a result of a fire in one of the new Wright R-3350 twin-row radials, each developing some 2,200 hp. To provide maximum high-altitude performance on this pressurized aircraft, each of the engines was fitted with a pair of turbo-chargers and reduction gearing to permit optimum propeller revolutions.

The B-29 was an extremely advanced aircraft for its time, a fact emphasized by the type's sleek lines and remotely-controlled armament, located in four barbettes above and below the fuselage to supplement the manned tail turret. The third prototype was extensively modified in the light of company and initial service trials, and then sent to Wichita, where B-29 production was slated to begin. It was in Wichita that the 14 pre-production YP-29s were built, followed by the first production models. Bell was also able to start production on time, and the third source came on stream when the US Navy's facility at Renton on Lake Washington was exchanged for the US Army's factory at Kansas City. Fisher Body became a major producer of sub-assemblies, its position in the production programme being taken by Martin at Omaha, Nebraska. One of the most impressive parts of the whole B-29 programme was the extent and smooth-running of the huge sub-contracted effort involved in this high-priority aircraft programme. Literally thousands of factories, large and small, were involved in the manufacture of single items or major portions of the airframe and its equipment, these being brought together in the right order and quantities at the four assembly facilities. But it was unavoidable that with an aircraft of the complexity of the B-29 there should be snags, and these were initially with the bomber's auxiliary equipment. The US Army therefore set up special modification plants at Kansas City, Marietta and Omaha to iron out these problems without upsetting the production lines. The US Army's lack of experience in this field was made worse by support problems and dismal weather for outside work, but during a six-week flurry of activity during March and April

1944, known as the 'Battle of Kansas', the first B-29s were made operational.

It had been decided that the B-29's range and armament made it a natural choice for Far Eastern deployment, and the type's first operational sortie was a raid on Bangkok from Indian bases on 5 June 1944. The story of the basing, maintenance and support of the B-29s in the Far East is an epic in its own right, but it is sufficient to say that from the end of 1944 Japan came increasingly under the thunderbolt of the steadily-growing B-29 fleets. There were operational problems, but these were straightened out, and Japan's cities, transportation system and factories were rapidly wiped out. To cap it all, the type was used to drop the atom bombs which ended the Second World War when they destroyed Hiroshima and Nagasaki on 6 and 9 August 1945 respectively. The B-29 continued in wide service after the Second World War, and was eventually supplemented by 371 B-50s, basically an improved and up-engined version originally designated B-29D and produced under the Boeing designation Model 345-2. Taller vertical tail surfaces were fitted, and the Wright radials were replaced by Pratt & Whitney R-4360 radials each developing 3,500 hp: maximum speed was increased from 365 mph to 385 mph at 25,000 ft, and range from 4,100 miles to 4,650 miles or more.

Always eager to exploit something which was good and already available, Boeing used what was basically the Model 345's wing in the prototype long-range patrol bomber flying-boat it built for the US Navy, as the XPBB-1 Sea Ranger (Model 344). The largest twin-engined flying-boat ever built in the USA, the XPBB-1 first flew on the 4,000 hp of its two Wright R-3350

Though it concentrated on B-17 and B-29 production in the Second World War, Boeing had sufficient design capacity left for other types.
***Right:* The XPBB-1 Sea Ranger was a magnificent patrol flying-boat which would have entered widespread service if landplanes had not already been available for the same task.**
***Inset:* The XF8B-1 was a powerful fighter-bomber prototype.**

radials on 9 July 1942. With a bomb-load of 20,000 lb and a theoretical endurance of 72 hours, the Sea Ranger was a formidable aircraft in its class, but production of an initial 57 PBB-1 production aircraft was cancelled when it became clear that existing landplanes could do the job just as well. It was with the end of the Sea Ranger programme that the Renton facility became available for B-29 production.

An oddity amongst Boeing designs of the Second World War period was the Model 400, of which the US Navy ordered three prototypes under the designation XF8B-1. Powered by a 2,500-hp Pratt & Whitney R-4360 radial driving a six-blade contra-rotating propeller unit, the Model 400 was a versatile carrier-borne attack aircraft, capable of 432 mph at 26,500 ft and with a range of 3,500 miles. Armament of the proposed production version would

have included six 0.50-in machine-guns or six 20-mm cannon, plus up to 6,400 lb of disposable ordnance in the bomb bay and under the wings. The first XF8B-1 flew in November 1944, and the type was the heaviest carrier-borne aircraft of the Second World War with a maximum take-off weight of 20,508 lb. The end of the war resulted in the cancellation of the type.

Discounting the experimental Models 344 and 400, and the Stearman-designed products of the Wichita Division, Boeing's 'meat' during the war had been the building of the B-17 and B-29 bombers. Production of the B-17 had been ended just before the end of the war in Europe, and while the B-29 was playing a decisive part in the struggle with Japan, Boeing's senior management was all too aware that the end of the Second World War was likely to mirror that of the First World War: wholesale cancellation of orders, bringing with them the prospect of lean times for all concerned with military aviation. Boeing's fears were nearly justified, for with the end of the war with Japan all B-29 contracts were cancelled, only those aircraft almost ready being completed. All Boeing's facilities closed down for a time as the wartime staff returned home, but by the end of 1945 the Seattle Division had again reached a strength of 9,000 personnel, needed for the B-50 and C-97 programmes. But Boeing was one of the least affected major aircraft manufacturers, for it was concerned with the production of heavy bombers of the type needed for the US Army Air Force's strategic arm:

Most extensively built model of the Stratofreighter series, the KC-97G was a versatile tanker and transport. The Boeing flying-boom refuelling gear is well displayed, together with its operator's position under the tail.

67

the last B-29s were delivered in May 1946, while the first B-50 flew in June 1947.

The company knew full well that gas turbine powerplants had revolutionized fighter design in Europe, and that US companies were rapidly developing American turbojets and turboprops. Once these new engines had reached maturity, a new generation of aircraft would be needed, but in the meantime Boeing had other projects which would, hopefully, keep the company profitably employed until the jet age got properly into its stride. The two most important of these stopgap projects were the Model 367 and the Model 377, both of them the result of Boeing's wisely-held belief in the reuse and adaptation of successful features, components and even whole assemblies. This aspect of the company's beliefs had stood Boeing in good stead in the 1930s, and was to do so again during the 1940s and onwards.

The Model 367 had a relationship to the Model 345 (B-29) identical with that of the Model 307 to the Model 299 (B-17): it was a transport using the wings, tail, powerplant and landing gear of the Model 345 combined with a new 'double-bubble' (vertical figure-8) fuselage to provide greater payload volume with a pressurized environment. Among the advanced features of the design were a loading ramp in the underside of the fuselage, and an overhead hoist to ease the movement of freight in the upper compartment, which was 74 ft long and could hold items such as trucks and light tanks as well as troops. The design was of immediate interest to the US Army Air Forces, and three prototype XC-97s were ordered in January 1942. The first of these flew in November 1944, and all three performed impressively during their service tests. In July 1945 the US Army ordered 10 pre-production aircraft: six YC-97s all but identical with the XC-97s; three YC-97As related to the B-29D (later B-50) with an airframe of stronger alloy, R-4360 engines and a taller tail; and one YC-97B similar to the YC-97As but finished as a VIP transport with freight capability deleted.

The USAAF opened its account for the C-97 with an order for 27 production examples of the Model 367, designated C-97A Stratofreighter and built under the company designation Model 367-4-19. Orders for the C-97A finally totalled 50, and the next freight type was the C-97C, of which 14 were built for use mainly as aero-medical evacuation aircraft during the Korean War.

Where the Model 367 really came into its own was as a flight-refuelling aircraft. Boeing's experience with this way of increasing an aircraft's range stretched back to 1929, when a Model 95, named *Boeing Hornet Shuttle,* had made several nonstop flights across the USA with the support of Model 40B-4s and a USAAC Douglas C-1 converted as aerial tankers. These early mid-air refuellings were successful, only because they used special pilots and were carried out in good weather. The experience of the Second World War showed that standard use of flight refuelling would prove very useful, both tactically and strategically, and Boeing developed the KB-29P version of the B-29, fitted with the Boeing-designed flying-boom system, in which the operator located in the tanker aircraft steered the refuelling boom (by means of a small butterfly-tail) into a receptacle on the aircraft that needed the fuel. Earlier experiments with a free hose system had proved only moderately successful, but the flying boom was a total success.

The system was first used with the Model 367 in the form of three C-97As modified under the designation KC-97A, and the combination proved itself well suited to the refuelling of B-50 bombers. The first proper production tanker was the KC-97E version of the C-97C. Production of this tanker variant totalled 60, and improved versions were the KC-97F (159 built) and the KC-97G (592 built), both convertible tanker/freighter models. Many other variants were produced, some of them only experimental, and the need for the tankers to keep up with ever faster combat aircraft resulted in the fitting of two turbojet boost engines in underwing pods on the converted KC-97L version. These engines, a pair of J47 units, were fitted

on the attachment points originally provided for auxiliary fuel tanks: this booster had been first used on the KB-50 versions of the basic B-50 family.

Boeing also proposed a civil version of the Model 345 from an early date. Although this had to wait for the end of the war, it soon appeared as the Model 377 Stratocruiser, based on the airframe of the YC-97A with the

Seattle
6,980 B-17

380 Douglas attack bomber

12 Model 314
10 Model 307
3 XB-29
3 Xc-97
3 XF8B-1
1 XPBB-1

Renton
1,119 B-29A

Wichita
8,584 Kaydet

2 XAT-15
1 XA-21
1,664 B-29

1 XBT-17
750 Waco CG-4A

Vancouver
362 Consolidated boats

17 Blackburn Shark
379 total

Douglas Aircraft
2.995 B-17F and B-17G

Lockheed Aircraft
2,750 B-174 and B-17G

Bell Aircraft
668 B-29 and B-29B

Martin Company
536 B-29

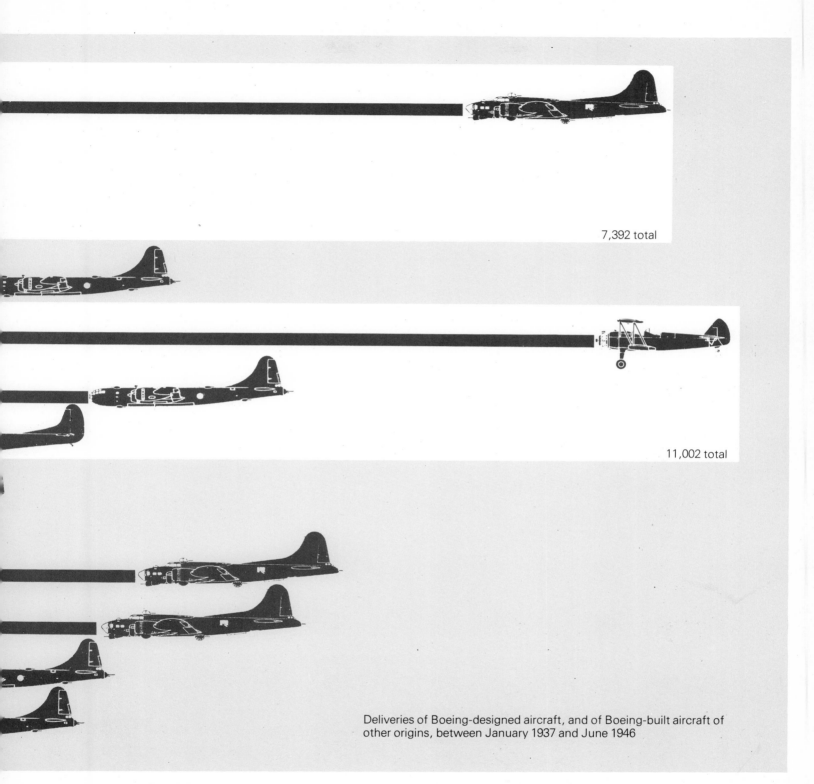

7,392 total

11,002 total

Deliveries of Boeing-designed aircraft, and of Boeing-built aircraft of other origins, between January 1937 and June 1946

interior of the YC-97B. Up to 100 passengers could be carried, and the type proved immensely popular for its spacious interior on two decks. The prototype (Model 377-10-19) flew on 8 July 1947, and production totalled 55 aircraft. This low figure is in part explained by the high cost of such an aircraft in comparison with the small sums charged by the US Army and US Navy for their masses of war-surplus transports.

Boeing's final piston-engined aircraft was the Model 451, a product of the Wichita Division, which had been kept barely alive after the war as a design group. The Model 451 was a careful design to provide the US Army with a utility scout/liaison aircraft having excellent fields of vision, good low-speed handling characteristics, and easy dismantling for air transport in the C-97. The prototype, designated XL-15 Scout by the US Army, flew on 13 July 1947, and was followed by 10 YL-15 service test examples. No further production followed.

THE AEROSPACE LEADER

Boeing diversified greatly during the 1960s and 1970s into a host of allied technological fields.

Above: The E-4B derivative of the 747 airliner is the world's heaviest, costliest and most powerful military aircraft – a survivable command post for the USA's civil and military administration in the event of a nuclear war.

Far left: Twin-rotor helicopters, like this Model 107, are the special province of Vertol, bought by Boeing in 1960.

Centre left: Boeing has also built prototypes for the US Army's General Support Rocket System, the trainable launcher holding 12 free rockets.

Left: Another Boeing speciality is the hydrofoil type of craft for a number of civil and military roles.

BOEING'S INTEREST IN gas-turbine powerplants began in 1943, when the company was asked, together with other manufacturers of combat aircraft, to consider how such a powerplant could best be used on military aircraft. The US Army Air Forces asked Boeing to produce a design study for a turbojet-powered medium bomber/photo-reconnaissance aircraft. Boeing's first effort was the Model 424, which resembled a scaled-down Model 345 (B-29) powered by four jets in pairs under the wings. The design then went through various stages to appear as the Model 432 with four engines buried in the fuselage. As this variant seemed to offer real possibilities, the USAAF awarded Boeing a research contract for further work, at the same time funding another four studies by other manufacturers.

At this time the war in Europe came to an end, and together with other countries the USA rushed to grab as much of Germany's secret technology as possible. So far as aircraft designers were concerned, the most important part of German aeronautical research was that dealing with swept wings, which could delay the formation of drag-producing shock waves as the aircraft approached the speed of sound. Boeing immediately reworked the design to include the most important parts of this new information, and then went back to the USAAF with its Model 448; which was based on a wing swept back at an angle of 35°. Though it thought that most of the revised aerodynamic design was good, the USAAF came to the unevitable and sensible conclusion that it was spoiled by its powerplant, which consisted of four engines buried in the fuselage: these would present two forms of trouble, for they would be difficult to maintain, and would also be very vulnerable to enemy fire in combat. Boeing agreed that this grouping of engines in one general place did present the operator with difficulties, and thought again. Finally the USAAF agreed with Boeing on the Model 450: this was powered by six engines mounted under the wings (in two pairs and as two singles), and was in most respects a highly radical design quite

apart from its wing and powerplant arrangement. Most notable of the Model 450's unusual features was an incredibly thin wing, which in turn meant that the main landing gear units had to be fitted as tandem 'bicycle' units under the fuselage, the aircraft being balanced on the ground by small outrigger units that retracted into the inboard engine nacelles. The basic Model 450 design was agreed in October 1945, just after the end of the war against Japan, and the USAAF placed a contract for two XB-47 prototypes in April 1946.

The prototypes were built in great

secrecy at Seattle, and the first XB-47 Stratojet caused an enormous stir when it was rolled out on 12 September 1947. The prototype was powered by six 3,750-lb thrust General Electric J35 turbojets, sufficient to give a sparkling flight performance that included a maximum speed of 578 mph. However, the slow acceleration of the turbojets of the time meant that the take-off run would have been enormously long if rocket assistance had not been provided, so the fuselage behind the wing was pocked with holes for 18 solid-propellant boost rockets, each developing 1,000-lb

thrust. The second prototype had 5,200-lb thrust General Electric J47 engines, and this considerably improved performance in this and later aircraft. Contemporary engines also had no thrust reversers (in fact still giving quite a high forward thrust even when idling), so the XB-47s were fitted with 32-ft diameter braking parachutes under the tail to shorten their landing runs. The B-47 series was classified as a a medium bomber type, with emphasis on the delivery of nuclear weapons. Such weapons were fairly large in the late 1940s and early 1950s, so the three-seat B-47 had a

massive bomb bay capable of accepting 10,000 of conventional bombs or, with modification, one 22,000-lb blockbuster.

Despite the complexity of the type, with its radar-controlled barbette-mounted tail armament of two 0.50-in machine-guns, testing was carried out quite smoothly, and soon involved 10 B-47A (Model 450-10-9) aircraft, which were service-test aircraft despite their production designation. The first true production variant was thus the B-47B (Model 450-11-10 and revised suffixes), of which 399 were built. Deliveries began in the middle of 1951,

The RB-47E (*foreground*) and B-47E gave the USAF unequalled reconnaissance and bombing capability in the 1950s.
***Inset:* A B-47A brakes with its parachute.**

making the US Air Force's Strategic Air Command a much more powerful and versatile force. In comparison with the bombers it was replacing in the medium-range role, the B-47 Stratojet could carry about the same load over the same type of range, but at very much faster speeds and with greatly increased chances of hitting

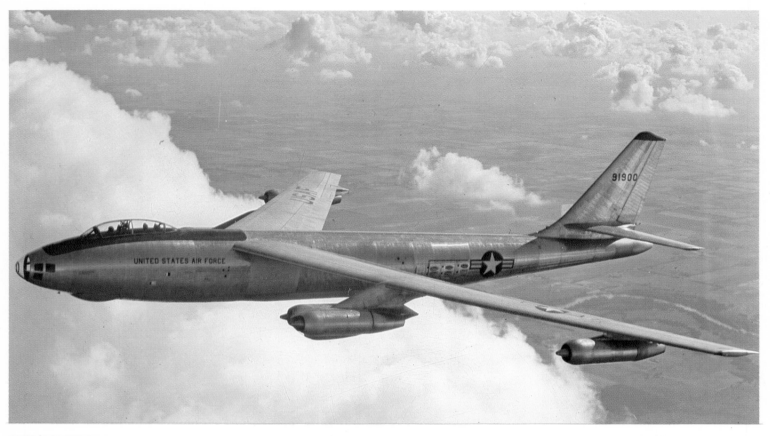

Above: The first B-47A shows off the type's thoroughbred, sleek lines.
Left: A B-52D, modified to carry 'iron' bombs in the tactical role rather than nuclear weapons in the strategic role, comes in to land at a Thai base during the Vietnam War.

the target thanks to the use of the latest radar-bombing techniques. All in all, the B-47 was perhaps the single greatest step forward in the history of bomber aircraft to date. The value of the B-47 is indicated by its production history, an overall total of 2,060 being built. This was beyond the immediate capabilities of Boeing, so the wartime consortium of Boeing, Douglas and Lockheed Vega (known within the aviation industry as BVD, in a humorous reference to the USA's most popular brand of men's underwear), which had built the B-17, was revived. The three companies' totals were 1,374, 274 and 394 respectively when production was completed in 1956. During its long service life the B-47 was considerably converted, modified and modernized in a whole series of variants, covering bomber versions, specialized photo-reconnaissance and electronic-reconnaissance

Above: **Carrying up to 75,000 lb of conventional weapons, the B-52 proved a devastating if uneconomical attack platform in the Vietnam War.**
Right: **A Boeing AGM-86B Air-Launched Cruise Missile drops away from its B-52 launch aircraft during trials.**

models, drone directors, guided-missile launch platforms, transition trainers for B-47 bomber models, radio-controlled drones, inflight-refuelling tankers, communications relay stations and a large number of experimental and test-bed models. The B-47 family reached its peak as a medium bomber with the B-47E version, which first flew in January 1953. Production of this definitive model reached 1,590 (931 by Boeing, 274 by Douglas and 385 by Lockheed), providing the Strategic Air Command with a versatile and fully developed aircraft for bombing and reconnaissance. Compared with the B-47B the B-47E had more powerful engines (six J47-GE-25 turbojets each rated at 7,200-lb thrust with water-injection), the internal JATO fit replaced by an external and jettisonable rack for 33 1,000-lb thrust rockets, tail armament improved to a pair of 20-mm cannon, ejection seats for all three crew members, and the nose revised to allow the provision of a socket for inflight refuelling. Maximum weight rose to 206,700 lb (compared with 140,000 for postwar B-29 models which could carry a greater bomb load), but speed was an impressive 606 mph at a height of 16,300 ft, range 4,000 miles and service ceiling 40,500 ft.

To partner the high-speed but medium-range B-47, the USAAF needed a longer-range heavy bomber, and in June 1946 Boeing was awarded funding for a preliminary study into such an aircraft. The difficulty was in providing the necessary performance: there was no problem in designing an airframe with the required load-carrying capability or range; but to combine these two factors with speed was another matter. Jet engines would of course provide the speed, but only at the expense of range, for contemporary engines were enormously thirsty: for a range of about 4,000 miles the B-29 had needed some 5,500 gallons of fuel, while for the same range the B-47 required no less than 17,000 gallons. The USAAF wanted turbine power, and so Boeing's initial Model 462 offering was a straight-winged aircraft powered by six 5,500-hp Wright T-35 turboprops. The USAAF turned this down on the grounds of inadequate range, so the design was modified to use more powerful, but more fuel-economical, versions of the same engine, with maximum take-off weight increased by 130,000 lb to 480,000 lb. The USAAF accepted this basic design and said that it would order XB-52 prototypes once the design had been finalized. The company was well aware of the design's limitations, however, and went ahead privately with plans for a pure-jet bomber to meet the same specification. This proved to be a farsighted move, for in October 1948 the US Air Force told the company that the turboprop-engined design was incapable of undertaking its required role, but that a revised design using the new and highly promising Pratt & Whitney J57 turbojet might meet the requirements. Working largely from memory in their hotel near Wright

Field, six Boeing engineers reworked the whole project as a swept-wing aircraft with eight J57s, and after only a weekend's work were able to show the US Air Force a revised specification and model. Official interest was revived, and two B-52 prototypes were ordered under the designations XB-52 and YB-52 (Model 464-67).

The first of these was rolled out in November 1951, and immediately impressed with its family likeness to the B-47, though vastly scaled up, with eight engines instead of six, and with a tandem main landing gear arrangement, though this last was based on two pairs of narrow-track legs to support the 390,000 lb maximum take-off weight. The Model 464 was completely re-engineered compared with the B-47, and had enormous growth potential thanks to its great volume and the pod-mounting of its engines. The XB-52 Stratofortress first flew on 2 October 1952, and was joined by the YB-52 and three pre-production B-52A (Model 464-202-0) aircraft in the next two years. Intense development work was carried out with these five aircraft, and the first true production aircraft was thus the B-52B (Model 464-201-3) with improved engines and all the system modifications that had been tested out in the first five aircraft. Full-scale production of the B-52 was now under way, and eventually some 744 were delivered by the Seattle and Wichita Divisions of the company. The type has proved itself beautifully adaptable, for though designed as a high-altitude nuclear bomber, it is now seen as a low-level aircraft capable of delivering free-fall bombs, stand-off missiles and cruise missiles. The powerplant and avionics have been completely revised, and the type also served in the Vietnam war as a conventional weapon with enormous loads of 'iron' bombs. There is every likelihood of the B-52 soldiering on into the twenty-first century in substantial numbers.

The final version of the Stratofortress was the B-52H, which brought into USAF service a whole run of improvements in this mighty warplane. Compared with the earlier models it has the great advantage of turbofan engines, which are really advanced

Above: **A Boeing 707-321 of Pan Am, the airline that was first to introduce the initial intercontinental version.**

Below: A USAF KC-135 tanker, refuels a flight of F-105 Thunderchief fighter-bombers. The KC-135 has a total capacity of 25,980 imperial gallons and can transfer fuel at the rate of 5,850lbs per minute.

Above: With the 'Dash-80' prototype Boeing proved the value of high-speed refuelling and opened up new horizons.

versions of the turboprop. But while the standard turboprop drives an ordinary propeller and also produces a little basic thrust, the turbofan produces more basic thrust and yet develops its main power in the form of a mass of air shifted backwards round the outside of the core engine by means of a large-diameter fan at the front of the engine and enclosed in a wide duct. The great benefit offered by such turbofans is a large reduction in fuel consumption compared with turbojets of the same power. And while the B-52G is powered by eight 11,200-lb thrust Pratt & Whitney J57-P-43W water-injected turbojets, the B-52H has eight 17,000-lb thrust Pratt &

Whitney TF33-P-3 turbofans to provide the same range but at the lower, thirstier altitudes at which the B-52H must operate to survive against modern missiles. This low-level flight requirement was also taken into account in the beefing up of the aircraft's structure, which in this last model has to stand up to much more buffeting in the turbolent lower air. But performance is still impressive, with a maximum speed of 630 mph at 40,000 ft, a range of 10,000 miles, and an armament of free-fall weapons, 20 SRAM stand-off missiles and, in revised models, the ability to carry the miniature AGM-86B Air-Launched Cruise Missile, also designed and built

by Boeing.

Given its early experience with turbine powerplants, it is hardly surprising that Boeing soon began to consider the turbine as the power for transport aircraft as well as combat aircraft. The starting point for these company feelings was the Model 367, in service with the USAF as the C-97. Large numbers of design studies were considered with the Model 367 as the starting

Right: The EC-135H is a flying command post for senior USAF officers in times of conflict.

Below: An E-3A Sentry Airborne Warning And Control System (AWACS) now serving with the USAF, NATO and Saudi Arabia.

point, and slowly this process removed all resemblance to the original aircraft. The decisive moment came with the Model 367-80 design. The basic promise of turbojet-engined transports had been confirmed by the pioneering de Havilland Comet, an unfortunate British airliner that encountered problems with metal fatigue, and Boeing took the enormously bold step of financing, as a company risk, the construction of a Model 367-80 prototype at the cost of $16 million.

The Model 367-80, which was rolled out on 14 May 1954, was a huge step forward for a transport aircraft, for it combined the advanced aerodynamics of the B-52 with the internal arrangement (sound-proofing, comfort and even luxury) of the Model 367/377 series and a new, sturdy structure to suit the type to the intensive airline use it would have to face. The four Pratt & Whitney JT3 engines were civil versions of the J57s used on the B-52, and these were slung under the wings in individual pods, leaving the wings themselves free for control surfaces and high-lift devices, making possible

the use of current airfields with little difficulty or loss of payload.

The Model 367-80 was airborne for the first time on 15 July 1954, and was immediately seen as 'a winner', but only if the company could afford to produce it. For Boeing's up-front investment had been sufficient only to build an aerodynamic prototype to prove the type's basic potential, and this prototype was never intended for service. Flight trials confirmed the company's hopes, and also interested the USAF, who saw in the type a replacement for the C/KC-97 series, which was approaching the end of its useful life. The company's gamble paid off when the USAF ordered the type into production under the designation C-135 (Model 717). Eventually some 820 examples of the military version of the Model 367-80 were built in a marvellous number of transport (C-135) and tanker/transport (KC-135) versions, soon multiplied into an enormous number of subsidiary variations for a wide variation of roles.

Production of the Model 717 allowed Boeing to recover its costs on the Model 367-80, and also financed

Above: Production of the Model 737 is undertaken by The Boeing Commercial Airplane Company at Renton to meet worldwide demand for this effective twin-engine short-haul transport. *Above and below right:* There is a commonality of some 60 per cent in structure and systems between the Models 727 and 737, resulting in lower unit costs.

the establishment of the necessary production lines. The first KC-135A flew on 31 August 1956, with deliveries to the USAF beginning on 31 January 1957. Before this, however, Boeing had achieved a decisive break into the civil market with the same basic type, marketed under the designation Model 707. USAF agreement had first to be gained for the company to proceed with the civil version, but once this had been granted the orders began to come in. Though closely related to the Model 717, the Model 707 in its initial form had a cabin 4 in wider and 10 ft longer, plus a completely different interior and avionics for the civil market. Designed for the US domestic market as a transcontinental aircraft,

the initial Model 707-100 (or -120) flew on 20 December 1957. Three aircraft were used in the intensive process leading to civil certification, which was given on 18 September 1958, allowing Pan American to begin scheduled operations with the revolutionary airliner on 26 October 1958, with a service from New York to London. Pan American and other early production Model 707s soon reverted to transcontinental rather than transoceanic flights, though Boeing later produced true long-range versions of the Model 707. Variants have been numerous, and by the end of its production run in the early 1980s the Model 707 had been built to the tune of some 808 examples.

The Model 707 also opened the way for a whole series of Boeing airliners designed to fill every part of the major airliner markets. The Model 720 was an intermediate-range development of the Model 707, with a revised wing planform, a shorter fuselage and totally revised structure, but proved only moderately successful in a production run limited to 154 aircraft. The Model 727 began its life before the Model 707 had flown, and was designed as a short/medium-range partner for the Model 707, with special provision for 'bus' operations involving rapid repetition of the take-off/landing cycle, with short turn-round times. Powered by three turbofan engines located in the tail, the Model 727 has proved the most prolific of Boeing civil designs. The first aircraft flew on 9 February 1963, and has by the early 1980s been followed by orders for an additional 1,800 examples. The Model 737, which first flew on 9 April 1967, is the baby of the family, and was designed as a twin-engined short-range transport. By the end of 1981 orders for the type totalled 969, with every prospect of further increases.

New life has been injected into the Model 737 series by the development of the Model 737-300, a 'stretched' version seating up to 128 passengers compared with the Model 737-200's 113 fare-paying passengers. More significant, however, is the fact that Boeing has been able to revise at low cost the structure of the aircraft sufficiently to accept a pair of new-technology

The Model 747 is a multi-capable aircraft able to operate in the passenger role, or in the freight role, or in the mixed passenger/freight role. Seen here is the specialized freight model, the 747-200F. This has an upward hinged door through which loads up to 8 ft 2 in high and 8 ft 8 in wide can be loaded. A wide variety of pallets, containers and bulk loads can be accommodated, and the special computerized handling system allows a mere two men to load the maximum payload of 254,640 lb in only 30 minutes.

turbofans (either the CFM56-3 or the Rolls-Royce/Japan RJ-500, each rated at about 20,000-lb thrust), which will burn some 20 per cent less fuel than the present Pratt & Whitney JT8D turbofans. It is expected that this latest version will enter service in about 1986.

Altogether different is the Model 747, the 'jumbo jet' and the world's heaviest aircraft. This was designed to carry some 500 passengers or an equivalent load of freight (in later models 248,000 lb) in a mammoth two-deck fuselage on the power of four enormously powerful turbofan engines. The family resemblance to other Boeing airliners is still there, but the scale of the Model 747 is of another order. The first example flew on 9 February 1969, and by the middle of 1981 orders stood at 575, of which 522 had been delivered. The Model 747 ushered in a new era in civil air transport, comparable with that brought in by the Model 707: while the latter ushered in the age of high-speed travel, the former pioneered the age of mass air travel at the same speed in a wide-body aircraft that offered spacious accommodation in an interior that also looked spacious. In some respects, therefore, the Model 747 may be considered the jet-age counterpart of the Model 377 Stratocruiser.

The high internal capacity of the Model 747 makes it a versatile aircraft, and this factor has made possible the Model 747-200B Combi, a special derivative of the basic Model 747-200B uprated passenger aircraft. The Combi is intended for mixed passenger/freight loads, and to this end a large door is incorporated in the port side of the fuselage aft of the wing. This measures 10 ft by 11 ft 2 in, and gives access to the main deck, which can accommodate an all-passenger load, or alternatively up to 12 pallets or containers of freight with a reduced passenger load separated from the freight by a movable bulkhead. Further growth of payload is catered for in the Model 747 SUD, produced in response to a Swissair demand. This Stretched Upper Deck can be fitted to all Model 747s except the Model 747SP, and increases the passenger capacity of the

small upper deck from 32 to 69 seats, a 10 per cent growth of capacity at the expense of a mere 2 per cent increase in empty weight.

And as the Model 707 was the structural basis for the E-3 Sentry AWACS (Airborne Warning And Control System) aircraft, with far-seeing radar in a rotating radome and sophisticated computer/communication gear to control national air efforts in either a conventional or a nuclear war, so the Model 747 is the point of origin for the E-4, which is a survivable but enormously costly airborne national command post to supervize the USA's entire war effort in the event of major hostilities. As a result of the project's huge cost, only a few E-4s have been built.

To a certain extent, the more recent Boeing airliners have been something of a problem when they entered service: for all that it was fitted with high-lift devices on its wings, the Model 707 could only develop its real abilities when longer runways were available, and the first success of the type soon persuaded the operators of the world's airports that the expense of extended runways would soon be recovered by increased traffic. And so it proved to be. The Model 747 introduced a different problem: its passenger capacity, about two and a half times that of the Model 707-320 intercontinental version, meant that airports had to deal with greater numbers of passengers. At first the problem seemed to have been overplayed, for only a few aircraft were in service, and the sudden arrival of perhaps 400 passengers could just about be catered for with existing facilities. But as more and more Model 747s entered service, airports found that the arrival of three 'jumbo jets' with some 1,200 passengers completely swamped facilities designed for only 500 or 600 passengers at a time. So the introduction of the Model 747 into widespread service saw a rash of airport extension. In overall terms, though, the introduction of the wide-body Model 747 and its successors (or rivals) has been of benefit, for each aircraft is more efficient than the 707 and the other airliners it replaced, allowing more passengers to be carried for less cost.

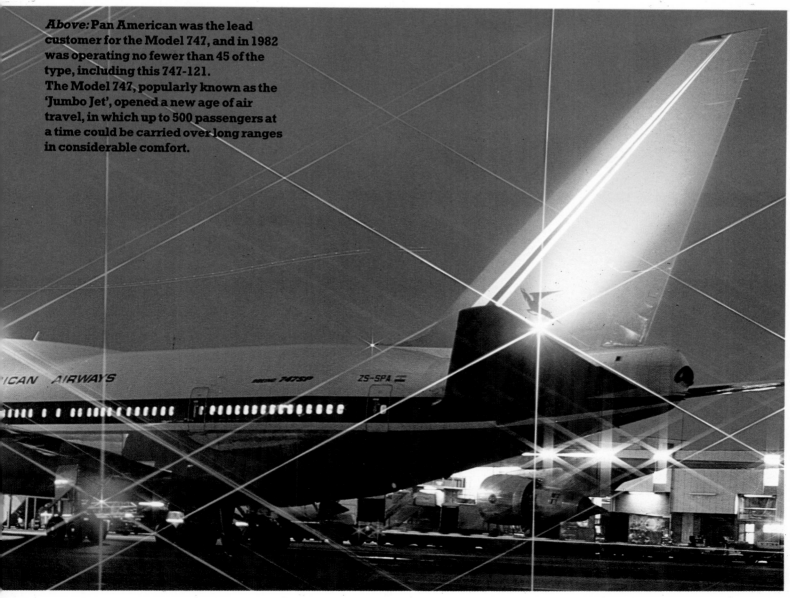

Above: Pan American was the lead
customer for the Model 747, and in 1982
was operating no fewer than 45 of the
type, including this 747-121.
The Model 747, popularly known as the
'Jumbo Jet', opened a new age of air
travel, in which up to 500 passengers at
a time could be carried over long ranges
in considerable comfort.

The company's two latest airliners are the Model 757 and Model 767, which are due to enter service in the first half of the 1980s. These are again similar to their predecessors, but offer a significant reduction in seat-mile costs thanks to careful design and engineering combined with computer-controlled flight management systems and fuel-efficient turbofan engines. The Model 757 may be regarded as the successor to the Model 727, in that it is a narrow-body airliner for short/medium-range operation, while the Model 767 is a wide-body aircraft for medium-range routes. The first Model 757 flew on 19 February 1982, while the Model 767 became airborne on its initial flight on 26 September 1981.

While the design and building of aircraft for the civil and military markets remained as the mainstay of Boeing's operations, from the 1950s onwards the company began to diversify its efforts into other fields, though these were generally related to the company's main occupation. This expansion of interests was recognized in 1961 by a change of name, The Boeing Airplane Company becoming The Boeing Company. Apart from aircraft, the company's main interests lay (as they still do) in missiles, spacecraft, gas turbine engines, hydrofoil craft and related topics such as windmills for the generation of electric power, to name but a single example.

Further restructuring of the company followed in December 1972, largely to meet the company's still-widening spheres of interest. Under the overall control of The Boeing Company, with its headquarters in Seattle, are The Boeing Commercial Airplane Company (headquarters at Renton), The Boeing Aerospace Company (headquarters at Kent, Washington), The Boeing Wichita Company (headquarters at Wichita) and The Boeing Vertol Company (headquarters at Philadelphia, Pennsylvania). The Boeing Commercial Airplane Company, as its name implies, is concerned with the company's airliners (support for earlier types, production of current types and design/planning of future types); The Boeing Aerospace Company is involved with

Boeing has doubled its options with its latest generation of airliners. The Model 757 (*left*) is a narrow-body type offering great economy of flight operation on short- and medium-range routes, while the Model 767 (*below left*) is a wide-body type optimized for medium-range routes. The first examples of the two made their initial flights in February 1982 and September 1981 respectively.
Above: Qantas, the Australian airline, operates two Model 747SP short-body airliners for very long-range routes.
Right: Production of the Model 747 continues at Everett outside Renton.
Below right: In-flight movies and the freedom to move about the aircraft have made the Model 747 very popular with passengers.

a host of products ranging from drone aircraft (remotely-piloted vehicles) via ground- and air-launched weapons, military aircraft and electronics, to spacecraft; The Boeing Wichita Company is concerned with the production of components for current civil aircraft and with the support of Boeing military aircraft already in service; and The Boeing Vertol Company, which was established in 1960 when Boeing bought Vertol (a pioneer in the development of twin-rotor helicopters), is the rotary-wing branch of the company, which builds and supports worldwide fleets of Model 114 and Model 234 helicopters, and also produces under licence a version of the Messerschmitt-Bölkow-Blohm BO105 utility helicopter. All in all, The Boeing Company is in an immensely strong position, and there is every likelihood that the company will continue to go from strength to strength, setting the pace for the rest of the world in its wide range of activities.

Boeing's association with rotary-wing aircraft is recent, and stems from the company's purchase of Vertol (itself a successor to Piasecki) in 1960, together with obligations for product support for the earlier types.

Left top: The Piasecki H-21 Workhorse was a SAR and utility transport of the 1950s, here seen with floats.

Left centre: The Vertol VZ-2 was a 1950s' tilt-wing research aircraft.

Left bottom: The US Navy's Piasecki HUP Retriever of the 1950s and 1960s was a piston-engined plane-guard and SAR helicopter.

Right: The Boeing Vertol CH-46 Sea Knight is a utility transport for the US Navy and Marine Corps.

Far right: The Model 234LR is the civil version of the CH-47 Chinook medium-lift military helicopter.

Centre: The Boeing Vertol YUH-61 was the unsuccessful 1970s' contender for the US Army's Utility Tactical Transport Aircraft System.

Below and bottom right: The Boeing Vertol CH-47 Chinook serves the US Army as a versatile and frequently updated logistic and assault transport.

Some of Boeing's designs have not
achieved the fame of products such as
the Models 707 and 747, though this is
not to say that the designs have been in
themselves unsuccessful.
Right above: The Aero Spacelines
Guppy-201 is a highly effective
adaptation of a Boeing design, in this
instance the C-97/Model 377 basic type.
Aero Spacelines evolved this monster
transport in the early 1960s for the
carriage of outsize booster rocket
stages for NASA and the US aerospace
industry. Since that time the Guppy
series has been developed with
turboprop engines, while the specially
designed bulged fuselage (with a nose
that swings completely open to allow
straight-in loading of long items) allows
the Guppy to carry such things as
complete fuselage sections of the BAC
One-Eleven airliner from the UK to
Romania, to which country production
is being successively transferred.
Right below: One of Boeing's most
ambitious and technically successful
designs has been the YC-14 contender
for the USAF's Advanced Military STOL
(Short Take-off and Landing) Transport
with extremely advanced
aerodynamics centred on the concept of
Upper-Surface Blowing for quite
exceptional STOL performance. The
project was killed for financial reasons.
Below: The Model 2707 was a project for
a Mach 2.7 airliner, but was cancelled
by political pressures in early 1971.

Boeing is of immense importance to the US defence forces, not only as the builder and technical prop of the B-52 bomber (one of the three main elements in the US 'triad' of primary strategic deterrents with its Boeing AGM-69A Short-Range Attack Missile and Boeing AGM-86B ALCM). Boeing is also the manufacturer of another 'triad' element, the Minuteman I.C.B.M.
Inset below: Boeing is also concerned with 'conventional' weapons such as the General Support Rocket System to provide the US Army with long-range 'artillery' support with potent rockets fired from mobile launchers.

It can fairly be said that by the 1970s Boeing expertise had spread to all types of transportation: land, sea, air and space, plus a host of related spheres. The part of the company responsible for trains for US urban transit authorities is Boeing Vertol, two of whose products are seen here.

Above: Rapid Rail Vehicles are in production for the Chicago Transit Authority.

Right: An example of the Light Rail Vehicle system is seen under test on San Francisco's celebrated hilly track layout. This type of train has been ordered by the urban transport bodies of Boston and San Francisco.

Hydrodynamics and aerodynamics are very closely related, and it is thus not surprising that Boeing's maritime efforts should have been concentrated on the hydrofoil type of craft, which 'flies' above the surface of the water on foils buried under the surface to provide lift.

Above: Final preparation for the launch in May 1981 of the USS *Taurus*, third unit of the 'Pegasus' class Patrol Combatant Missile (Hydrofoil). Waterjets powered by an 18,000-shp gas turbine give this craft a foilborne speed of 48 knots. Armament is very powerful: eight Harpoon surface-to-surface missiles and one 76-mm gun.

Left: HMS *Speedy* was a Boeing commercial hydrofoil evaluated by the Royal Navy as a possible patrol craft, but was withdrawn from service in 1982 mainly as a result of financial cutbacks.

Boeing is currently involved with a number of far-sighted projects.
Left: An experimental wind-driven generator, its rotor spanning 300 ft on a 200-ft tower, develops 2.5 megawatts.
Immediately below: Impression of a generating system using reflectors to concentrate sunlight in the tower.
Below: Impression of a four-unit orbiting solar power station.
Bottom left: The WASP mini-missile would be a potent tank-destroyer.
Bottom right: The 'stealth' bomber would have virtually no radar 'signature'.

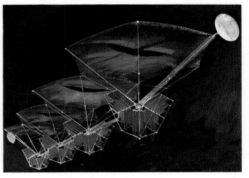

INDEX

The researchers and publishers would particularly like to thank Mr Thomas Cole of the Boeing Commercial Airplane Company, Mr James Grafton of the Boeing Aerospace Company and Ms Madelyn Bush of the Boeing Vertol Company in the USA and Mr D Kenney in the UK for their invaluable help with the pictures for this publication.
Unless otherwise indicated below all material was supplied by Boeing.
Artworks: Pierre Tilley
British Aerospace p90
British Airports Authority p82-83
British Airways p2-3
Delta Airlines Inc p81(top)
S Howe p62, 63
M Jerram p34-35
Pan Am p76-77(top), 83(centre)
Qantas p87(left)
US Air Force p48-49, 51, 53, 54(btm), 55(top), 55(btm), 61, 62-63, 74(btm), 75(top), 76-77(btm), 91
US Navy p54(top)
Vosper Thornycroft (UK) Ltd p93(btm)